**Joanna Bawa, Pat Dorazio
and Lesley Trenner (Eds)**

The Usability Business

Making the Web Work

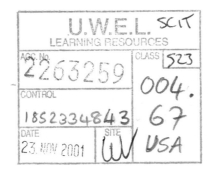

 Springer

Joanna Bawa
IT Consultant, Watford, Hertfordshire

Pat Dorazio
SUNY Institute of Technology, USA

Lesley Trenner
GlaxoWellcome Medicines Research Centre, Gunnels Wood Road, Stevenage,
Hertfordshire

British Library Cataloguing in Publication Data
The usability business: making the Web work.
   (Practitioner series)   1. System design 2. Human-computer interaction
   I. Bawa, Joanna II. Dorazio, Pat III. Trenner, Lesley, 1957–
   658'.05
   ISBN 1852334843

Library of Congress Cataloging-in-Publication Data
Bawa, Joanna.
   The usability business: making the web work/Joanna Bawa, Pat Dorazio and
Lesley Trenner.
      p. cm. – (Practitioner series)
   Includes index.
   ISBN 1–85233–484–3 (alk. paper)
   1. World Wide Web. 2. System design. 3. Management information systems. I. Dorazio, Pat,
1953– II. Trenner, Lesley, 1957– III. Title. IV. Practitioner series (Springer-Verlag)
TK5105.888 .B39 2001
658'.054678–dc21   2001042664

Practitioner series ISSN 1439–9245
ISBN 1–85233–484–3 Springer-Verlag London Berlin Heidelberg
a member of BertelsmannSpringer Science+Business Media GmbH
http://www.springer.co.uk

Typeset by Florence Production, Stoodleigh, Devon, England
Printed and bound by the Athenæum Press Ltd., Gateshead, Tyne & Wear
34/3830–543210 Printed on acid-free paper SPIN 10834532

Series Editor's Foreword

Following the success of the 1998 Practitioner Series book *The Politics of Usability* by Lesley Trenner and Joanna Bawa, it was an easy decision to agree to produce an updated version. However, the changes in the subject have been so fast in only three years, that we have this excellent new book *The Usability Business: Making the Web Work* instead of a second edition of the first book. And we welcome the addition of Pat Dorazio to the book editorial team.

The Practitioner Series does not make a habit of publishing an edited book, but *The Usability Business: Making the Web Work* is an example of a subject area that is probably impossible to cover effectively any other way. We have already observed the dynamic nature of the material, but the latter also spans all aspects of computing from human factors to hard technology. To do justice to the range and the rate of change of the subject requires the collective expertise of active practitioners and hands-on researchers which is exactly what the book offers. There are 25 contributors to this book made up as follows:

Practitioners   12
Practitioners who were formerly academics 3
Academics who were formerly practitioners 2
Hands-on academics   8

So this is clearly a Practitioner Series book for practitioners (and hands-on academics) written by practitioners.

Whilst technology continues to advance at amazing speed (or is it my age!), we have too many disappointments when the technology is used. One reason for this is that determining how a system should work is difficult. It is this fundamental problem that *The Usability Business: Making the Web Work* addresses. The book has several running themes such as "you can never over-explain an idea" and a three-part structure in which to cover the material. The first part looks at political and practical difficulties experienced by consultants and practitioners. It is consoling at least to know that one's personal professional difficulties are shared! The second part looks at the increasingly wide range of application areas. And the third part concentrates on the Internet, whose growing pervasiveness now encompasses almost all usability issues.

I normally finish my series editorial with a recommendation as to whom the book should be read by. I find it difficult in this case, because who should *The Usability Business: Making the Web Work* not be read by? I recommend this book to all practitioners, academics students, and other people wishing to be knowledgeable. If anyone reads the book and learns nothing, please let me know on ray.paul@brunel.ac.uk

I do not expect to hear from anyone!

Ray Paul

Preface

In a world where technology companies rise from the dust, flare briefly and brilliantly, then crumble away again, leaving a vast army of devastated investors and a tiny handful of millionaires in their wake, we're entitled to ask – what happened? Time and time again, great technology ideas turn into great technology disasters, and no one really knows why. The likelihood is that every flop had a multitude of reasons for its failure and that no two companies suffered from the same combination of circumstances. Nervous sponsors, cash-flow problems, inadequate research, over-ambitious targets, and not enough skilled staff are routinely cited as factors in high-tech failure, and all of them probably contribute. It's a fast-changing, unpredictable business, with a huge number of unknowns. Making technology work seems to be a very hard thing to do.

This book is for the people who are trying to make technology work by ensuring that adequate time, money and intellect is spent on researching, understanding and responding to the needs of the human users of technology. Their contribution to each successful product is a small fraction of the total effort of the product team, and in the past it's probably not even been the most important one. That, however, seems to be changing. In recent years, the job of liaising between technology and human has literally exploded in terms of its scope, depth, breadth and range. The range of people who consider some sort of user awareness to constitute part of their job description has expanded enormously; the same is true of the disciplines which are now actively contributing to the bodies of knowledge variously known as usability, human-computer interaction, cognitive ergonomics, human factors, user experience or user-centric design. It's important that we know more about ourselves and our relationship with technological systems, because the economic fact is stark: a successful product is not one which does what it claims to do, which "works" – it's one which is used. Understanding how a product "works" – or not, is relatively straightforward; understanding why it is used, liked or adopted – or not – is not.

And that's where we come in.

Welcome to *the Usability Business: Making the Web Work*. A follow-up to *The Politics of Usability*, this book is for anyone who has ever tried to find out whether the technology project they're working on has a viable future.

Joanna Bawa

Contents

Introduction

No sooner is the ink dry on the page of a book about usability, than something new needs to be said. Thus it was always clear that when *The Politics of Usability* was first published in 1998, it could not hope to cover the full spectrum of issues with which its title is concerned. Indeed, with its emphasis on laboratory testing and the quest for "satisfaction, efficiency and effectiveness", it was written and read by those most concerned with business applications and user productivity in the workplace. While this remains at the core of much professional usability activity, it now occupies a smaller proportion of our efforts.

Back in 1998, usability practitioners were already deeply involved in trying to understand "New Media" and its role and potential in our lives, both professional and personal. But what exactly is "New Media"? Like so many high-tech buzzwords, it can be hard to define, but for the purposes of this book, if 'Old Media' is radio, television, land-line telephones and print, "New Media" is everything else which allows us to acquire new information. Mobile phones, wireless and infrared technology, CDs, e-mail, connected personal organizers, interactive TV, intranets, and of course, the overwhelming, dominant, all-consuming Internet. It's a lot for one industry to be working on, and a huge challenge for the small group of usability professionals within that industry.

Where once we were called upon to ensure that a software program enabled the maximum level of work with a minimum of frustration, now we are called upon to evaluate and comment upon the "richness" of knowledge in an intranet, the "wow factor" of a home page, the "desirability" of a telephone handset, the "power" of a brand, the "experience" of web interaction, the usefulness of e-mail on television sets – and many similar questions which haven't even yet been clearly articulated. Technology has become a pervasive presence, and our role as mediator between it and ourselves has expanded accordingly. Almost overnight, the sharp divide between business and home technologies has disappeared. The most powerful PCs now sit in spare bedrooms, not in executive offices; a CD is more likely to hold an electronic game of breathtaking sophistication than a database; television viewing has given way to online surfing; e-mails, images and text messages are sent and received by our children and our grandparents with equal ease. Businesses are digital, shopping takes place online, trading is electronic and gadgets are

wireless. It makes for a pretty overwhelming new world to live and work in – indeed, it's now an e-world – and usability professionals are among those at the forefront.

Designing technology so that it fits in with our lives, our minds, our diverse individual preferences and our unpredictably peculiar eccentricities is a task which will never be complete. Not only does the technology keep changing, but so do the needs of its users – and the users themselves. Even to refer to them as "users" seems rather arcane – they are customers, clients and consumers; they are actors, interactors; even experiencers. Whatever they may be, there is growing recognition within the organizations that these creatures are vital to the success of new technologies, and that their views must be understood and taken into account. User research and product usability have matured and "arrived", the proportion of technology companies which employ no one with some usability expertise is small and dwindling. At one level, the battle has been well and truly won.

But acceptance as a valuable resource is just the beginning for usability professionals. The range of technologies we use every day is vast, and growing all the time, and our ways of interacting with it are changing and developing in ways which cannot be anticipated, but which can affect the very foundations of society. It is an awesome undertaking to define what constitutes a "good" experience, to attempt to evaluate someone's level of enjoyment, or to design a sophisticated consumer technology product which will please everyone, and be used by everyone. Nevertheless, this is exactly what usability professionals across the world are doing, and as these chapters show, they are doing it with flair, imagination and daring.

That politics remain a feature of our professional lives is inevitable. When a discipline enters the mainstream of corporate life, it becomes subject to the same forces as every other discipline already there. Usability activities can no longer rely on the protection of a "champion" to ensure their survival – they must be justified and paid for, they must be defined and distinguished from other activities, they must be made to show results. While our track record of product improvement and its indirect relationship with profit margins means we may no longer have to fight for every penny, it is our misfortune that so much of usability is concerned with the intangible and the unquantifiable. A historical preoccupation with usability metrics has undoubtedly contributed to the quality of many technology products and has probably been a major factor in the greater acceptance of usability as legitimate corporate research and development activity. Even so, there are those who argue that an excessive focus on measurement has sidelined the importance of experience and emotion in a person's response to a technology and turned

usability research into little more than a "black box", in much the same way that BF Skinner attempted (unsuccessfully) to reduce psychology. Luckily, New Media has solved this for us.

The vast range of communication, leisure and consumer technologies which fall into the category of New Media are often less tools than they are toys. In their capacity as consumers, "users" are not interested in achieving goals or producing end results. As consumers, they want to have fun. Some companies now offer products which, they claim, will "delight" those who buy them; many offer an "experience" or a lifestyle, rather than a product. Not even the toughest executive can continue to argue that emotion is irrelevant to technology, and that's true in the hard-nosed corporate market as it is in the consumer market. Intranets, for example, aren't about servers and networks, they're about the sharing of knowledge, which in turn is about power and politics. The process and the technology may be there, but if people feel threatened or insecure by sharing their knowledge, it won't happen. Identifying an emotional/cultural problem like that won't be done by the hardware people, the software people or even the content managers; it will be done – and probably solved – by the usability people, in whatever guise they are working, as long as they are allowed to study how people "feel" about their intranet.

The Usability Business: Making the Web Work shows how far we've come from error counting in the Usability Lab, all the way to refining and influencing the very emotions our users /clients /experiencers feel before, during and after their interaction with technology. This move towards the broader "experience" of a user demonstrates most clearly how much our own discipline is beginning to grow and overlap with others. Throughout this book there are references to ethnographers, anthropologists, social and cultural experts, marketers, brand experts, change managers and project managers, even style consultants and trend-setters, all of whom are contributing to the field of usability. From one point of view this may seem threatening, with our little pool of expertise about to be washed away in a tidal wave of other interdisciplinary contributors. On the other hand, it's no longer realistic to expect that a body of knowledge called human factors, usability, or human computer interaction (HCI) can answer every human question which technology raises. Instead, as the technology spreads and expands into every aspect of our lives, so does the expertise required to understand and manage it. We need to know more – or at least, learn to work with others who know different things.

And if you're suddenly feeling overwhelmed at the sheer enormity of the task as a usability consultant, it's worth observing that a core of common principles remain as true today as they did ten years ago. Throughout the following

chapters, several themes recur. It still pays to secure support from senior management, especially when there are no guaranteed results; you can never over-explain an idea (the scope for misunderstanding is infinite); numbers, statistics and percentages are never enough without the support of interpretative "soft" data; and now, truer than ever, if a customer can't do what they want with your technology, they'll just go somewhere else. Clarity of purpose, understanding of the user, an awareness of the distinction between *big picture* and *fine detail*, the ability to communicate clearly, constructively and consistently to groups who don't always want to hear, and the political skills to steer a product in something other than its original direction – these remain the core skills at the heart of our profession.

Like any dynamic discipline, usability continues to grow and change – sometimes through mergers with other disciplines, sometimes through a fundamental new realization or understanding of the way people adapt to and interact with technology. It can be confusing and frustrating, but it's also a tremendous challenge and a busy crossroads between fields inspiring some of the best intellectual effort in industry today. So, just as it looks like we've captured some reliable truths about the best way to design an interface, or position a button, or colour an icon, the goalposts change again. These "principles" now constitute a tiny fraction of the library of knowledge we need to draw upon to do our jobs properly – which means we're back at the beginning again, but this time in a much bigger pond.

About This Book

This book is divided into sections which attempt to reflect the core issues and technologies which are affecting the practice of usability within organizations today. Part 1 deals with some of the difficulties we often experience in our capacity as consultants and practitioners, both political and practical. Part 2 of the book takes a look at the enormously diverse areas in which usability professionals are now working and what political skills we need to continue growing our role without losing its focus. In just a few years, usability expertise has expanded way beyond technology and is now routinely used in organizations specializing in anything from tourism and leisure to history. We may still be working with the interface between human and technology system, but the way we do so has changed in many profound ways. Finally, Part 3 concentrates on the Internet, both as the publicly available Web and in its private incarnation as the intranet. Internet technologies are so immensely important that they have already ceased to be an issue in themselves, but simply gone directly to a position as the keystone of modern communications technology. Directly and indirectly, the Internet is now generating almost all the issues with which usability professionals are now dealing.

In **Part 1** of the book, **William Mitchell** and **Heather Heathfield** begin by highlighting the stark contrast between the values and objectives of HCI research and usability activities within academia versus the "real world". Whatever knowledge you acquire during the rigorous training which an academic HCI degree affords, they suggest, you can be certain it won't be enough to get you through a genuine project unscathed. Key to this observation is the realisation that one activity is about furthering knowledge, the other is about furthering sales. This may seem obvious, but moving out of the ivory tower (even if only temporarily) is an increasingly popular choice being made by HCI academics these days. This in itself is encouraging – the sophistication of today's new technologies demands sophisticated knowledge – but it's also true that those new to the practice of usability need to acquire a whole secondary armoury of knowledge to help them through the political minefields.

What happens when, halfway through a web-site usability evaluation, it becomes apparent that your client has no idea who their customers are? Or that the reason no one is buying their products online is that the name of the web-site doesn't quite match the name on the High Street? It's not so unusual to bump up against such major flaws, and though these are problems which a usability professional might well pick up, they might equally be spotted by the brand manager, the marketing consultant or the product manager. And when such a problem is discovered, whose responsibility is it to correct it? The boundary between usability activities and a range of other professions is sliding, changing and disappearing. After a lifetime of acquiring our expertise in one field, the world of New Media seems to require that we become experts in everything. This dilemma is eloquently expressed by **Tim Westall**, the only author whose core expertise is not in usability. A brand and marketing consultant, Westall has been asked for usability advice by clients who have a problem with their brand, and for consumer research when it's clear that the web-site design is atrocious. Part of our responsibility to our clients is to guide them towards a better understanding of the question, Westall argues, before we then attempt to answer it. And if we can't answer it ourselves, we need to form partnerships and associateships with those who can. Having already increased the level of usability research his own organization is carrying out, he suggests that the astute usability expert will ally and integrate with other experts in other disciplines, in order that both – and their clients – can benefit.

The "dot-com" downturn may have hit investors hard, but everyone is affected when an entire industry experiences the sort of roller-coaster ride that computing has seen lately. Keeping your usability consultant head above water when employees all around are drowning is the subject of **Jose Coronado's** chapter. His account of one organization's dramatic growth, restructuring and relabelling will be familiar to many of us, and his experience as a usability consultant throughout is enlightening. Starting from informal, out-of-hours beginnings, his team of usability engineers achieved formal status as a department just in time to be merged with another organization's human factors team, which was then restructured into small teams assigned to work with individual business units. His tips on surviving and thriving on such upheaval are welcome.

On a similar note, **Avi Parush** guides us through an increasingly common problem facing usability professionals – the frighteningly steep learning curve consultants must now climb in order to meet typical project planning schedules. Some technologies are so new or complicated that not even their designers fully understand them – what hope do we, as external consultants, have of formulating an authoritative opinion in just three months? Parush stresses the need to define and agree project requirements well in advance, since they may well change halfway through, and to develop new testing methodologies if required. The clever part, he reveals, is persuading your client that extensive preparatory work will reduce the total project time, rather than extending it.

Moving into **Part 2**, **Patrizia Marti's** chapter is a fascinating account of research into the behaviour of visitors to a museum of fine art in Siena, Italy, and their response to a new tourist-oriented technology. Each volunteer was given a sophisticated handheld electronic tour guide to take around the exhibits and asked to report back on their experience of using it. Normal usability metrics simply did not apply to this project, and Marti and her associate, **Paola Lanzi**, describe an ingenious technique for gaining useful information. Users were encouraged to provide feedback by "telling stories" within a structured framework, providing a rich soup of emotional, cultural and sensory material with which to inform subsequent design. A remarkable read in its own right, this chapter is also a fine example of the ways in which usability research is intermingling with many other disciplines, while retaining its own core purpose and approach.

While Marti and her colleagues are applying technology to our understanding of the history of fine art, **Phil Turner** and **Susan Turner** are dealing with the future of a technology which, just a few years ago, was science fiction. Their experience of evaluating a virtual reality system takes us deep into the usability issues associated with three-dimensional simulations and the ways in which we interact with them. Role-playing users wearing headsets and represented by avatars collaborated to extinguish fires, recover from floods and avert human conflicts – without a hint of help from Lara Croft. What sounds like a fantasy role-play game is an all-too-real and extremely serious training system, designed to train senior staff in the maritime and offshore sectors to manage safety-critical situations. Turner and Turner were asked to analyse how to get the most out of this collaborative virtual environment, while at the same time preserving the reality of an emergency situation. It led them directly to a question few of us would like to have to answer but will increasingly have to think about – just how real is real?

Similar questions, albeit in a different context, have been routinely addressed to **George M Donahue** in his role as an "XModeler". The term "XMod", a contraction of "Experience Modelling", is the title of a large group within a large organization, and may well be the largest group ever assembled with the sole purpose of studying and understanding "the user experience". Using techniques derived from the social sciences, marketing and HCI, XMod has gone far beyond straightforward interface design and instead is aiming for an entirely seamless approach to the holistic experience of using technology. The bringing together of so many disciplines echoes the themes expressed by Westall in his call for greater cooperation and understanding between related (and increasingly overlapping) bodies of knowledge, but as Donahue explains, it is not without its problems. Large and ambitious visions are admirable, he says, but cannot succeed unless they can be translated into specific projects, which can in turn be translated into specific tools and techniques (plus ça change). This means better definition of terms such as "experience" and the greater involvement of those with core expertise – such as usability engineers – in determining the strategy and direction of such an effort.

If designing an experience for adult users is hard, imagine the difficulties associated with designing for children. In his entertaining chapter, **Mike Pringle** describes the evolution of a highly sophisticated system, delivered over the Internet, via an interface incorporating friendly and intuitive virtual reality models. Intended to appeal to anyone with an interest in history and national heritage, the system encountered the full range of political obstacles – lack of sponsorship, poor awareness of the benefits of usability within the organization and a wide and ill-defined audience. Pringle's account explains how his team used a range of political skills to overcome these obstacles so successfully that the project almost acquired too many sponsors, creating another political challenge. In the end, however, an intelligent 12-year-old saved the day.

In Pringle's chapter, as in several others, the prototype is shown to be a very useful tool for trying out ideas before a full commitment is made to them. The political significance of the prototype is the main theme of the chapter by **Nick Bryan-Kinns, Magnus Lif, Fraser Hamilton** and **Ismail Ismail**, whose work in the design of large and extensive web-sites relies heavily on prototypes. Bryan-Kinns and his colleagues describe how prototypes ranging from paper-based sketches through to working web pages can be used successfully – or not – to persuade and explain. A prototype gives an impression, and while this is an ideal way to convey complex ideas to clients, it is also a means to enable clients, coders and users to impose their own agendas on incomplete snapshots of the final system, leading to divergent perceptions and political tension. In order to be useful, Bryan-Kinns et al. conclude, a prototype must facilitate shared understanding between different audiences – which means that one prototype may not always be enough.

In **Part 3**, the focus is almost exclusively on the web and its corporate sibling, the intranet. **Rob Procter, Scott Gallacher** and **Robin Williams** provide a classic tale of the twists, turns and political shenanigans which accompanied the implementation of an intranet within a large banking institution. In a large organization used to having power, they point out, few decisions are taken without the input of many senior executives, many of whom have directly conflicting interests. Progress is made through much deal-making and trading-off of needs and wants, budgets and savings programmes – and the fundamental requirements of the system's users often get pushed into second place. Procter and his team describe the ways in which they retained a focus on their professional objectives despite the opposing pressures of other parties, and also consider a slightly greyer area – how best to ensure that the inevitable political wrangling above your head can be made to work in your favour.

The power and passion surrounding intranets is equally well illustrated by **Lucy Suits** and **Lee Zukor**, whose chapter covers a similar area to that of Procter et al., but with a very different focus. Providing insights from their work as an external consultant and an in-house employee respectively, Suits and Zukor describe the ways in which those who should most often be cooperating are most often those at war. Reflecting other themes in the book which reveal the blurring of disciplinary boundaries, this chapter shows knowledge management experts, information systems project managers, graphic designers, marketing leaders, HTML developers, and usability engineers fighting for their places in an intranet project, each convinced that they know best. It's not that any of them are wrong, Suits and Zukor point out, it's just that when it comes to making intranets work, nobody really knows what the best thing to do is. When it comes down to young disciplines working with immature technologies, the best way forward seems to be to take as active a role in the preparatory work at as early a stage as possible. Political skills are vital for achieving unity and consensus, and for setting manageable, realistic goals which can provide a reward for as many people as soon as possible. Only then, they conclude, can long-term creativity and the impact of high quality usability work become apparent.

The political pressures at the intersection of the web and usability is highlighted by **Karen Gunter** in her chapter on the vital task of homepage design – and how to get people beyond it. Her work on an EU-funded web project to support small rural communities throughout the European Union turned up an entire raft of conflicting needs and objectives. Multiple languages, multiple stakeholders and multiple purse-holders were all powerful influences in the development of a cross-border web service, intended for a user group with relatively little experience with technology. Gunter's work on the project's interface and usability shows how seemingly intractable conflicts can be overcome by identifying tiny problems which everyone can agree need solving, then developing themes to work on – such as user research, navigational structure, information structure or prototype development – which follow logically from these tiny problems. Her chapter is also an abject lesson in the politics of dealing with bureaucracy. Few high-tech organizations have been around long enough to acquire established processes or rigid mentalities, but growing numbers of their clients have. Gunter's tips on persuading and selling to bureaucracy, and ultimately working gracefully within its constraints, should be taken to heart by all of us. She also makes the very salient point that can be easy to forget: however bad a web-site may appear, its problems are almost never the result of carelessness or indifference, but of someone's sincere belief that what they are doing is the best way to proceed for that particular circumstance.

Finally, we return to the cutting edge of the Internet with **Richard Anderson** and **Jared Braiterman's** expansive chapter on achieving user-centred design within the high pressure world of e-business. Two very experienced consultants, Anderson and Braiterman draw on their work with a wide range of clients, ranging from tiny all-digital start-ups through to huge corporations reluctantly converted to the web as a means of doing business. Perhaps unhappily for the rest of us, the authors do not offer a neat set of principles which can be readily applied to the development of a user-centric e-business projects. Rather, they emphasize the profound differences that organizational culture and context bring to bear, now that e-business is relevant to all sorts of organizations within every sector, and that we must learn some things afresh, at least to some extent, with every new client. Once again, however, a core lesson of their experience is the need to think creatively and go beyond the traditional parameters of usability, delving into a wider range of related disciplines in order to find comprehensive answers to complex questions. They also stress the need for self-knowledge in determining our own values, preferences and biases, as well as our areas of weakness where we could do more to improve our own knowledge and awareness.

The Business of Usability: Making the Web Work isn't a detailed recipe for dealing with the huge number of complex new issues we're encountering all the time in our professional lives. Instead, it's a rich cross-sectional account of the kinds of situation usability professionals can expect to deal with sooner or later, and some of the lessons learned by those who have already been there. In a discipline where an understanding of human nature within a technological context is so central to our success, there can be no simple answers – nor indeed, any answers which remain consistent across time or organization. But such is the nature of our work, and in this collection of chapters, we hope you will recognize your own situations and find something new and useful to take away.

March 2001   *Joanna Bawa and Pat Dorazio*

Author Biographies

Anderson, Richard

Richard is well-known for his teaching and his support of the development of communities around the world to improve the practice of experience research and design. He is the Local SIGs Chair for ACM Special Interest Group on Computer-Human Interaction and long-time Program Chair for the San Francisco Bay Area chapter (BayCHI).

Until the high-tech economic downturn led to Viant's slashing half of its workforce and closing several of its offices, Richard Anderson was a Digital Agenda Leader at Viant and head of Viant's Experience Center. Richard provided guidance and direction to Viant efforts at "partnering" with customers and potential customers of Viant's clients in order to develop the deep understanding of customer experience necessary for designing innovative, customer-centered businesses and business offerings.

Prior to joining Viant, Richard started and led the User Research and Experience Strategy discipline at Studio Archetype and Sapient. He has also worked as an independent consultant providing usability and user-centered design and discovery services to a wide range of clients. Before that, he worked as a human factors specialist at a telecommunications company and as a teacher and researcher at the University of Illinois.

Contact:
Richard Anderson • E-mail: riander@well.com

Bawa, Joanna

Joanna Bawa is a human factors psychologist and writer, specializing in the interaction of people with an increasingly technological working environment. Her work is concerned with the development, not only of technology products, but with entire systems which support human, rather than business, needs.

She began her career as a human factors engineer with British Telecom, studying the way in which we learn to interpret icons and how best to present complex information in a simple way. This led to a spell as a professional technical communicator, before joining the launch team of PC *Magazine UK* in 1992. Here, Joanna established a laboratory method for comparing the usability of competing software and hardware products.

Joanna now works as an independent consultant and writer, exploring the issues which are becoming increasingly important as technology becomes a greater part of our lives. Living in a computerized environment, she believes, depends on our ability to recognize our unique strengths and weaknesses as human beings and then adapt technology to accommodate us – rather than the other way around.

Contact:
Joanna Bawa   •   Tel: + 44 (0)1923 249633   •   E-mail: jobawa@aol.com

Braiterman, Jared

Jared Braiterman, Ph.D. works to make innovative applications pleasurable and simple. He guides executives and product teams in learning directly from customers and aligning strategy, technology and end users. Research methods include ethnography and iterative testing.

Jared led Experience Design at Shutterfly, an online digital print service, from 1999 to 2001. He has also introduced ethnography and customer-centered design at Small Pond Studios, Sapient and Studio Archetype.

Jared has worked in technology design since receiving a Ph.D. in Cultural Anthropology from Stanford University in 1996. Clients include Hewlett Packard, EXPN, Leap Frog, REI, Electronic Arts, Industry Standard, Listen and Schwab Foundation.

Contact:
Jared Braiterman   •   E-mail: braiterman@acm.org

Bryan-Kinns, Nick

Nick Bryan-Kinns is a Usability Engineer whose core skills in identifying user requirements and establishing user interface design are vital to Icon Medialab's client activity.

In addition to working on projects, Nick is developing best practice in the HCI area for Icon Medialab. This includes a publishing project for 2001 and the development of HCI conferences by the London office.

As well as lecturing in Graphical User Interface Design, Nick researches the design, analysis and evaluation of multimedia-based collaborative support tools. His special interests are in human computer interaction, interactive video and understanding human behaviour. This has led to academic journals publishing his papers, one of which he also presented at the HCI 2000 conference. He is highly qualified in the area of Human Computer Interaction with a PhD, MSc and a BSc accredited to his name.

Contact:
Dr Nick Bryan-Kinns • Icon Medialab London, Classic House,
1 Martha's Buildings, 180 Old Street, London EC1V 9BP •
E-mail: nickbk@acm.org

Coronado, Jose

Jose Coronado is responsible for the Usability Engineering division at Hyperion Solutions, a leading provider of business analytic application software. He has refined and developed the practical application of usability methods and techniques based on over 8 years of experience in interface design and human computer interaction. He received his master's degree in Industrial Design from the University of Kansas. He has published several papers, including recent work in remote usability evaluation and global interfaces.

As a usability consultant, Jose has lead the design and development of projects that have focused in augmenting the efficiency, productivity and usability of products for the telecommunications, software and hardware industries. He has also collaborated with other human factors consulting firms to develop and deliver web and GUI design training in the US, Canada and Latin America.

Contact:
Jose Coronado • Hyperion Solutions Corporation, 900 Long Ridge Road,
Stamford, CT 06905, USA • Office tel: + 1 203.703.3884 •
Fax: + 1 203.329.6729 • E-mail: jose_coronado@hyperion.com

Donahue, George M

George Donahue is a usability professional and writer living in Atlanta, USA. He has facilitated scores of usability tests of e-commerce, financial, interactive television and New Media web-sites. His current research interests include strategic usability and cross-cultural user-interface design. He has degrees from the University of Delaware and Clemson University. He edits *The Voice*, the online newsletter of the Usability Professionals' Association. He's also a member of ACM SIGCHI.

Contact:
George M Donahue • E-mail: george.donahue@mindspring.com

Dorazio, Pat

Patricia Dorazio is a tenured faculty member at SUNY Institute of Technology at Utica/Rome specializing in online information design and usability testing. Prior to joining the college, she worked as an Information Developer with IBM, responsible for redesigning an online HELP facility for a mainframe computer system, and was part of Corporate Education, responsible for curriculum in Interface Design. She is principal of PATent Solutions, a technical communication consulting company, and contributes to professional conferences and scholarly journals. Her outside interests include travelling, downhill skiing and gardening.

Contact:
Pat Dorazio • Communication and Humanities, SUNY Institute of Technology, School of Arts and Sciences, Donovan Hall/2131, Utica/ NY, 13504–3050 • Tel: + 1 315 792 7315 • Fax: + 1 315 792 7503 • E-mail: fpad@sunyit.edu

Gallacher, Scott

Scott Gallacher is an IT consultant whose professional career has focused on initiating, building and shaping organizations dedicated to the delivery of user centric e-business solutions. Scott's contributions to ensuring efficient and effective user experiences span a variety of roles including hands on development, technical architecture and executive project leadership. A key component of his expertise is his multidisciplinary educational background spanning business studies, computer science and sociology.

Scott currently holds the position of VP/Associate Director of Consulting Services with Digitas, a marketing and technology consultancy providing solutions for global blue chip clients including AT&T, General Motors, Xerox, American Express and Kingfisher.

Prior to his appointment, Scott served a variety of roles within the Professional Services organization for an e-commerce software provider, Intershop Communications. As well as growing this practice within the UK, he served in Developmental and Project Managerial roles and helped establish the Consulting practice as Manager for Technical Consulting. During this period Scott led engagements with key global projects for clients including Wella, Shell, Motorola and the Company's flagship site Homebase. His leadership on the Homebase project, their most complex installation, was instrumental in it being the recipient of many awards, including runner-up for site of the year in *Internet Magazine*. This work has provided him with a rounded and rich understanding of differing usability requirements amongst a range of target user groups.

Scott graduated from the University of Edinburgh with a BComm in Business Studies followed by an MSc in Human-Computer Interaction from Heriot Watt University. Scott wrote his dissertation on the usability evaluation and redesign of a Property Finders site by Callegrafix, a site later presented as their best work to *Internet Business* magazine. This was followed by enrolment for a PhD entitled "Implementing Multimedia Innovations in a Corporate Environment" at the University of Edinburgh. As part of his research, he performed a wide range of design, developmental and usability work on a number of banking systems. He is currently completing his thesis.

Contact:
Scott Gallacher •   Tel: + 44 (0)207 494 6873 •
E-mail: sgallacher@digitas.com or gallacher_scott@hotmail.com

Gunter, Karen

Karen Gunter works as the usability consultant for Amaze Ltd (a design and e-services company with bases in the UK and Germany). Her current role involves: the definition and provision of commercially appropriate usability and user-centred design services for a range of customer needs; the promotion of usability within the company through usability seminars (with speakers from industry and academia) and the pursuance of research collaborations.

Dr Gunter has substantial experience in the area of collaborative technologies with an emphasis on web based solutions. She has a PhD in computer science awarded by Manchester University and an MSc in data engineering.

Previously Karen worked as a usability consultant both as a freelance and for ICL Ltd. Her specialism is web usability which came about through her research interests and her role as a multimedia consultant. She originally studied Fine Art at the Slade School.

Contact:
Dr. Karen Gunter • Amaze Ltd, Port of Liverpool Building,
Pier Head, Liverpool, L3 1BZ • Tel: + 44 (0)151 237 1000 •
Mobile: + 44 (0)7887 606063 • E-mail: karen@nimm.demon.co.uk or
k.gunter@amaze.com

Hamilton, Fraser

Fraser Hamilton is a usability engineer and member of the Human Computer Interaction (HCI) team at Icon Medialab. He has designed innovative interfaces for e-commerce clients, undertaking user-requirements analysis, user-interface design and user evaluations. From a research point of view he has interests in developing principles of human-computer interaction, methodologies, supporting tools, user modelling, personalization and affective computing.

Prior to joining Icon Medialab Fraser was a lecturer at Brighton University, and before that he was part of the world-class HCI research group at Queen Mary and Westfield College (London University). He has published several academic papers and has presented his work in the UK, continental Europe and North America. He published a book chapter last year on cutting-edge techniques for user requirements analysis and modelling.

Contact:
Fraser Hamilton • Icon Medialab London, Classic House,
1 Martha's Buildings, 180 Old Street, London EC1V 9BP •
E-mail: fraser.hamilton@iconmedialab.co.uk

Heathfield, Heather A

Heather has worked as an academic in computer science for more than 15 years, specializing in the areas of user-centred design, human computer interaction and system evaluation. A strong theme in all her work has been the practical application of academic tools and techniques to real-world situations. Many of the applications she has worked upon have been in the healthcare domain, a particularly diverse and complex area for system design.

For the last 4 years Heather has been the director of IT Perspectives (ITP) Ltd, a consultancy company that offers a range of services including requirements work, interface design and evaluation. Through ITP, Heather has been involved in a range of large-scale projects working with Internet companies, system suppliers, the National Health Service, and the pharmaceutical industry. Her experiences have taught her that in the real world, an academic perspective can be of benefit, providing structure and rigor to system design and evaluation. However, as a consultant, she recognizes the difficulty of acting as a mediator between the client and system users, and has long since abandoned any illusions of objectivity.

Contact:
Dr Heather Heathfield • IT Perspectives Ltd, 27 Velvet House, 60 Sackville Street, Manchester M1 3WE, UK • Tel: +44 (0) 161 237 3005/ (0) 7956 288 565 • Fax: +44 (0) 161 236 1109 • web-site: www.it-p.co.uk • E-mail: it.perspectives@virgin.net

Ismail, Ismail

Ismail has degrees in Computer Science and Ergonomics and recently joined the Human-Computer Interaction team at Icon Medialab from University College London.

Contact:
Ismail Ismail • Icon Medialab London, Classic House, 1 Martha's Buildings, 180 Old Street, London EC1V 9BP • E-mail: i.ismail@totalise.co.uk

Lanzi, Paola

Degree in Communication Science at the University of Siena, Italy. Since August 2000 she has collaborated with the Multimedia Communication Laboratory of the University of Siena working on international projects for the evaluation of safety critical applications and nomadic systems for art and entertainment.

Her current areas of interest are air traffic control and information/activity design applied to art settings.

Contact:
Paola Lanzi • Department of Communication Science, University of Siena, Via dei Termini 6, I-53100 Siena, Italy • Tel: + 39 0577 286833 • E-mail: lanzi@media.unisi.it

Lif, Magnus

Dr Magnus Lif is the Chief HCI Officer at Icon Medialab London (IML). He has 7 years' experience in user-centred design of graphical user interfaces and has been with Icon Medialab, an e-business consultancy, for 2 years. At IML he has worked as an HCI consultant in several large e-commerce projects and has also been involved in developing strategies for user-centred design and integrating methods for analysis, design and evaluation into Icon Medialab's development model. Before starting at IML he finished a PhD in HCI at Uppsala University in Sweden. He has published several articles and book chapters focusing on the integration of HCI methods into the software development process.

Contact:
Dr Magnus Lif • Icon Medialab London, Classic House, 1 Martha's Buildings, 180 Old Street, London EC1V 9BP • E-mail: magnus.lif@iconmedialab.co.uk

Marti, Patrizia

Patrizia Marti is lecturer in Educational Technologies at the Communication Science Department of the University of Siena (Italy) and in Cognitive Ergonomics at the Industrial Design Department of the Polytechnic, Milano (Italy). She has been involved in international research projects in the areas of nomadic systems, educational technologies and air traffic control. Her current research interests include the design of human activities in context (situated interaction). In the past, she has been involved in the evaluation of different kind of systems, from complex, safety critical applications to everyday life objects applying a range of different methodologies. Currently she is interested in defining new evaluation methods to adopt in the field of art, entertainment and leisure where human activities are situated and "non-goal oriented".

Contact:
Patrizia Marti • Department of Communication Science, University of Siena, Via dei Termini 6, I-53100 Siena, Italy • Tel: + 39 0577 270335 • E-mail: marti@media.unisi.it

Mitchell, William L

William Mitchell has worked in the area of Human Computer Interaction (HCI) and interface design for over 12 years. In his "ivory tower" role he is a Senior Lecturer in the Department of Computing and Mathematics at Manchester Metropolitan University. He started off in research in the area of interface design for special needs users. For the last 5 years he has been investigating the use of new media in museum education. He is leader of the Virtual Museum Group at MMU (http://www.docm.mmu.ac.uk/ RESEARCH/virtual-museum). He has worked with Internet-based technologies, virtual reality and collaborative virtual environments.

In his "real-world" role he has provided consultancy for both public sector (education, museum, health) and private sector organizations. He believes in a very practical approach to requirements gathering and evaluation. Through his experiences he has an in-depth understanding of the problems of introducing processes to companies that ensure a satisfying user experience.

Contact:
Dr William Mitchell • 21 Bowers Street, Manchester, M14 6SU, UK • Tel: +44 (0)7710 664942 • E-mail: B.Mitchell@totalise.co.uk; B.Mitchell@mmu.ac.uk

Parush, Avi

Avi Parush has a background in cognitive experimental psychology, with MA and PhD degrees from McGill University, Montreal, Canada. He has been working in the field of human factors engineering since 1983, specializing in the area of human computer interaction and worked in various industries as both an employee and as a human factors group leader. Most of the time he worked as a user interface design and usability testing consultant to high-tech development companies. Experience includes working in domains such as command and control systems, fighter cockpit, printing, medical imaging, semiconductor manufacturing, web applications, cell-phone applications, speech-based interfaces and information visualization. He co-founded LaHIT, one of the leading user interface consulting firms in Israel, and has taught courses and workshops on user interface design in the industry, army, and universities. He presently has a visiting scientist appointment at the Technion, Israel Institute of Technology, where he teaches and conducts user interface design research.

Contact:
Avi Parush, PhD • Technion, Israel Institute of Technology, Haifa, Israel 32000 • Voice: 972–4–8294548 • Mobile: 972–50–429865 •
E-mail: parush@tx.technion.ac.il

Pringle, Mike

Mike Pringle is an Information Systems designer specializing in human computer interface issues, with particular emphasis on user-centred design. Mike has an extensive background in graphics and the presentation of information, including web-based design and Virtual Reality; and, holds a PhD in Computing Information Systems Engineering, gained through research into HCI development whilst at the Department of Informatics and Simulation, within the Royal Military College of Science, Shrivenham, UK. Mike has, for the last 18 months, held an advisory role within English Heritage, where he is concerned with matters relating to the Internet and other New Media technologies. During this time he has also been responsible for the specification, construction and implementation of a novel, VR-based interface (called PastScape), that has been designed to enable the public to access complex heritage datasets (across the Internet) without any training or knowledge of the underlying terminology.

Contact:
Mike Pringle • E-mail: mike@pringle.org

Procter, Rob

Dr Rob Procter is a senior lecturer in the Division of Informatics, University of Edinburgh and a member of the Institute for Communicating and Collaborative Systems. His research interests lie in the field of interactive systems design with the aim of understanding how non-technical issues: i.e. cognitive, social and organizational factors help shape processes of interactive systems design, development and application, and how they may be implicated in the success or failure of a specific system or innovation.

Rob Procter has held grants from SERC/ESRC Joint Committee, EPSRC, SHEFC and EC TAP. Current funded research includes dependability issues in healthcare informatics, a field study of applying user-led design and development methodologies, and social learning processes in IT systems implementation. He has published over 50 book chapters, journal and conference papers in the field of interactive systems design. He is a co-author of *Expertise and Innovation: Information Technology Strategies in the Financial Services Sector*, Oxford University Press, 1994 (with Fincham et al.). His other recent publications include:

McKinlay, A Procter, R and Gallacher, S (2001) The Influence of Network Quality of Service Factors on the Usability and Effectiveness of Multimedia Internet Broadcasting. In: Sloane, A and Lawrence, D (eds) Multimedia Internet Broadcasting: Quality, Technology and Interface, Springer, London, pp. 35–52.

Hartswood, M, Procter, R, Rouncefield, M and Sharpe, M (2000) Being There and Doing IT: A Case Study of a Co-Development Approach in Healthcare. In: Cherkasky, T, Greenbaum, J and Mambery, P (eds) Proceedings of the CPSR/IFIP WG 9.1 Participatory Design Conference, New York, 28 November–1 December 2000.

Trading Places: A Case Study of the Formation and Deployment of Computing Expertise (1998) In: Faulkner, W, Fleck, J and Williams, R (eds), Exploring Expertise. MacMillan, London, pp. 197–222.

Contact:
Rob Procter • Institute for Communicating and Collaborative Systems, Division of Informatics, University of Edinburgh, 80 South Bridge, Edinburgh EH1 1HN, Scotland • Tel: +44 (0)131 650 2707 Fax. +44 (0)131 650 6513 •
http://www.informatics.ed.ac.uk/people/staff/Robert_Procter.html •
E-mail: rnp@dai.ed.ac.uk

Suits, Lucy Mae

Lucy established her independent practice in July 2000. Before becoming an independent consultant she worked for Plural, an interactive consulting firm. At Plural, she established usability checkpoints throughout the design and development process, developed information architectures and conducted usability evaluations at all levels. Before working with Plural, Lucy founded the Usability Services Group at Wells Fargo Services Company. She is currently working on a large web application for a client in Minneapolis.

Before working in the field of usability, Lucy's career was in technical training and development. After years of developing training interventions, she made the move to usability, so she could be closer to the design and development process. "I love the field of usability; the role of user advocate and the opportunity to work with technology is a wonderful combination. It is the best of both worlds!"

In the year 2000 Lucy founded the first local chapter of the international organization Usability Professionals Association and is currently Past President of that organization.

Contact:
Lucy Mae Suits •   Suits and Associates, 80 Seymour Av SE,
Minneapolis, MN 55414 •   Business Tel: 612–220–6523 •
Alternate Tel: 612–378–2957 •   E-mail: l.suits@att.net •
UPA MN website: http://mouseworksmedia.com/upa/

Turner, Phil

Dr Phil Turner is a senior lecturer in the HCI research group of the School of Computing at Napier University after having worked for almost 10 years on a number of European-funded research projects during the 1990. At present his main research focus is the use of activity theory to provide a theoretical framework for HCI and user centred design. Phil is responsible for the requirements work on the DISCOVER project.

Contact:
Dr Phil Turner •   HCI Research Group, School of Computing,
Napier University, Edinburgh, EH14 1DJ, UK •
E-mail: p.turner@dcs.napier.ac.uk

Turner, Susan

Dr Susan Turner has been a researcher in HCI and CSCW (Computer-Supported Co-operative Work) since the late 1980s in a variety of industrial and academic contexts. She is a lecturer in the HCI research group of the School of Computing at Napier University, where her interests lie in the human aspects of collaborative technologies and the development of techniques to better support the user centred design process. Susan currently leads the evaluation work for the ESPRIT DISCOVER project.

Contact:
Dr Susan Turner • HCI Research Group, School of Computing,
Napier University, Edinburgh, EH14 1DJ, UK •
E-mail: s.turner@dcs.napier.ac.uk

Westall, Tim

Tim is a director of the strategic marketing consultancy, New Solutions, part of the Omnicom group of companies. New Solutions works with around 20 of the biggest brands in the FTSE 100, advising on branding and marketing issues. The firm comprises marketers, researchers and creatives, working in a uniquely collaborative and integrated way.

Tim is a classically-trained marketer, having spent 7 years in international marketing management roles with Unilever and ICI. He has lived in France and speaks fluent French.

He moved into marketing consultancy in 1994, working on brand development challenges across a wide range of sectors including food, drink, retail, leisure, financial and professional services.

For the past 2 years he has been leading New Solutions' e-marketing offer. This has involved the set-up of a specialist "qualitative usability lab", combining focus group and usability techniques in order to better understand online consumer needstates, attitudes and behaviours. In turn, this has helped many clients make the transition from online "shovelware" to more user-centric experiences that people actually like to visit more than once.

As an ex-engineer converted to marketing, Tim has a rabid belief in the need for the e-community to put the user far more at the centre of its thinking, breaking free from the technology-obsessed solipsism that characterises 90 per cent of the online world.

Contact:
Tim Westall • New Solutions, 14–15 Manette St, London W1D 4AP •
Tel: +44 (0)207 434 3535 • E-mail: taw@newsolutions.co.uk

Williams, Robin

Robin Williams is Professor of Social Research on Technology and Director of the Research Centre for Social Sciences/Technology Studies Unit at the University of Edinburgh. His interdisciplinary research into "the social shaping of technology" has focused upon the interplay between "social and organizational" and "technical" factors in the development and implementation of a range of technologies including Electronic Commerce/EDI, Production Management/Planning, Banking systems and EFTPoS. More recent work has focused upon the development and use of multimedia in business and in everyday life.

His interdisciplinary research collaboration with computer scientists includes the social science component of a European Commission (FP5/IST) Research and Development project: ParcelCall: developing an integrated logistics management system and the EPSRC-funded £6.8 million Dependability Interdisciplinary Research Collaboration at Edinburgh and four other UK universities which addresses the social and technical origins of undependability and how they may be tackled.

He has published several books in this field including: Expertise and Innovation: Information Technology Strategies in the Financial Services Sector, Oxford University Press, 1995 (with Fincham et al.); The Social Shaping of Information Superhighways: European and American Roads to the Information Society, Campus Verlag, 1997 (co-edited with Kubicek and Dutton); The Social Shaping of Computer-Aided Production Management and Computer Integrated Manufacture, 1997 (co-edited with Clausen); and was guest editor of a special edition of *The Information Society:* on *ICT Development and Use in Europe*, Vol. 16, No 4, Oct–Dec 2000.

Contact:
Robin Williams • Research Centre for Social Sciences, University of Edinburgh, High School Yards, Edinburgh EH1 1LZ, Scotland •
Tel. +44 (0)131 650 6387 • Fax. +44 (0)131 650 6399 •
E-mail: r.williams@ed

Zukor, Lee

Lee Zukor leads the Usability and Design Team at Best Buy Company, Inc., the United States' largest electronics retailer. In this capacity, Lee has worked with intranet and Internet sites, interactive kiosks, cash register applications, telephone call scripts, call centres and a variety of web applications. Lee managed the usability tasks related to Best Buy's intranet redesign in 2000.

Prior to co-establishing Best Buy's Usability and Design team in 1998, Lee worked as a technical writer with several large health care companies. He is a member of the UPA.

Contact:
Lee Zukor • E-mail: lee.zukor@bestbuy.com

PART 1

Usability Professionals: Dealing with Organizational Politics in an Uncertain World

The Myth of Objectivity: Making the Transition from Ivory Tower to Real-World Usability Evaluation

William L Mitchell

This chapter contrasts the purity of evaluation conducted in an academic environment with the political compromises that need to be made in real-world commercial evaluation. We begin by examining evaluation in an academic context and the importance placed on objectivity. We then contrast this with a case study from our first experiences in commercial consultancy which involved the evaluation of a community intranet. We outline some common mistakes of the first-time consultant, and how these can be overcome by learning to make clear viewpoints and affiliations in order to work constructively with both clients and users. We conclude with a series of lessons for those who may be thinking of making a similar transition from ivory tower to real-world evaluation.

Introduction

Academics involved in usability and evaluation studies strive to be objective and unbiased in their work. However, as any consultant working in the real world knows, such aspirations are unfeasible given the political nature of system design, and the differing agendas of users and developers.

At one level there are many similarities between the academic and commercial contexts in which evaluation takes place. Both academic and commercial projects follow a certain lifecycle (requirements, design, implementation). There is a focus on a product (a piece of software). At various points in the lifecycle this product is evaluated and a set of results produced. However, as we will show below, there are crucial differences.

Evaluation in the Ivory Tower . . .

What distinguishes evaluation in an academic context is the degree to which it is driven by intellectual objectives. There is an emphasis on being objective when evaluating. The particular evaluation method used must be justifiable and defendable. The results have to be shown to be repeatable.

Objectives of a Research Project

In an academic context, evaluation takes place as part of a project which is primarily driven by research aims. In research, the emphasis is on contributing to knowledge by discovering new or novel findings. The end goal is not a software product but rather a theory or model, which can lead to an academic publication.

Role of Evaluation

In a research project, a software product is developed in order to help develop and test a theory. The purpose of evaluating the product is to gather results, which can be used to develop the theory. Evaluation thus plays a key role in the design and planning of the research project.

Stage in the Life Cycle

Because it is clear what role evaluation is to play in the project, it is possible to precisely identify in advance at which stages of the project life cycle to carry out evaluation.

Constraints on Evaluation

As evaluation plays such a key role in the research project, it can be allocated an appropriate amount of time and budget. A large amount of time is devoted to analysis of evaluation results.

Subjects Used in Evaluation

In an academic evaluation, the recruiting of subjects is under the control of the researchers. In some cases this means using subjects who are willing to cooperate and can afford the time. In other cases the subjects may not be "real" users. For example, university students are often used to stand in for "real" users.

Type of Results Gathered

In usability research, there are two main trends in evaluation. The first is strongly influenced by cognitive science, where there is an emphasis on laboratory-based, controlled experiments. In this form of evaluation the results can be somewhat narrowly focussed and quantitative in nature.

The second trend is towards field studies, particularly ethnographies. Here the emphasis is on studying users in their everyday environment. What is of interest is the wider environment in which people operate and the details of their activities. In such a case, the results can be quite broad but very detailed.

How Results Are Used

As noted above, the aim of research is to generate novel findings, which are publishable. The results of evaluation are abstracted and generalized from in order to create publishable findings. These findings can tend not to be very practical in that they do not suggest actions or solutions for particular situations.

Audience for Results

The results of research are aimed mainly at academic peers. They tend to have quite a long life as they are published in journals, which may have significant lead-times for publication.

In order to contrast the academic context with the commercial, we next outline a case study drawn from our experiences in commercial consultancy.

. . . and in the Real World

In this case study we will outline some evaluation work we carried out as commercial consultancy. We have changed the names of participants to respect confidentialities.

Our client was CopperStone, a small start-up company that specialized in developing community-based intranets. In addition to the infrastructure (communication links, servers) they also provided front-ends for end-users. One such intranet had been developed for a local government authority. The intranet was targeted at members of the local authority community such as managers, administrators and workers. CopperStone was developing a new version of the intranet and had commissioned a software company (Orb) to carry out the development work. As part of this, CopperStone wanted a usability evaluation of the intranet.

The case study will show how we had to adopt varying roles and stances during the course of the work. This was necessary in order to manage our relationships with the other stakeholders in the project: CopperStone (our client), the local authority (CopperStone's client), Orb (the developers contracted by CopperStone), and the members of the local authority community (the end users of the intranet).

Winning the Chance To Evaluate

Our initial effort was spent on bidding for the work. We adopted what we now recognise as a somewhat objective, academic stance in convincing CopperStone of the need for evaluation, basing our argument mainly on the need to take user views into account in order to make a better product. We suggested that we should be part of the on-going development of the new system, and outlined in some detail the methods we would use and the justifications for using them.

We were making what are common mistakes for first-time consultants. We had spent a considerable amount of time bidding for the work (5–6 months), but did not succeed until we took a less purist line of argument. We had to change the emphasis of the bid from a justification of evaluation methods to an emphasis on the deliverables and benefits (particularly economic) to be gained from evaluation.

Our next problem was in agreeing a programme of work. CopperStone had not agreed to the budget outlined in the bid but instead asked us to carry out an evaluation worth a third of the original budget we had suggested. It was unclear who the results of the evaluation would be aimed at or whether we were supposed to evaluate the old system or to validate the design for the new version. Attempts at clarifying the situation proved fruitless. CopperStone seemed to have no clear idea about the role evaluation should play in the project or indeed the role we should play as evaluators. What was starting to become clear was that it would be up to us to define our own role in the project.

Shifting Roles: Who's Doing What with Whom?

Our first day of work involved a meeting between ourselves, CopperStone, and Orb (the company who would be implementing the intranet). We soon realised that CopperStone had not only failed to clearly define our role as evaluators but had also not clearly defined Orb's role. Orb had attempted to define their own role to some extent by preparing a functional specification of the new system before we had even had a chance to evaluate the old version of the system. Things became even worse when, during the meeting, CopperStone and Orb attempted to draw up a screen design for the new system.

No real work had been done with the users at this point. Therefore, to gain some control over the process, we suggested that we could carry out a more formative evaluation that could be used to influence the development of the new version of the intranet. We also provided Orb with a conceptual design of the new system in the shape of a set of functional requirements and screen designs.

A further shift in our role occurred when we tried carrying out user evaluations. We had had problems obtaining a list of users from CopperStone. We instead had to recruit users ourselves by making contact with members of the local authority community. It soon became apparent that we would have to abandon the idea of evaluating the old intranet as it was simply not being used by the community. This was because the developers of the exiting intranet had not understood the ways in which the community communicated and had imposed their own functionality on the community. To avoid repeating this mistake, we decided to shift the emphasis when meeting with users, from evaluation to requirements gathering. We tried to understand the community members and their existing ways of communicating with each other, effectively transforming our role into that of user advocate.

Our recognition of this user advocate role was to prove crucial in our next meeting. We had arranged to meet representatives of the local authority who had commissioned the intranet from CopperStone. From the start of the meeting it was clear that the local authority were not happy with the existing intranet and were in no mood to see the same mistakes repeated in the new version. The local authority representatives were sceptical about us and wanted to establish "whose side we were on". We had to be careful in deciding what position to take. On the one hand we had a duty to our client (CopperStone). On the other hand we fully understood the local authority's concerns as they echoed our own views as professional consultants.

By adopting the role of user advocate we were able to achieve neutral political ground and avoid being seen as representatives of CopperStone. In our earlier meetings with users, we had been able to gain their trust because one of our team had extensive knowledge of the local authority domain. This domain knowledge again played a part in winning the trust of the local authority representatives, and placed us in a new role as intermediary between CopperStone and the local authority.

The Aftermath

Over the course of this project we underwent several shifts in role – a process which political astuteness can minimise. This had a substantial impact on the content and structure of the evaluation report we produced. In our roles as user advocate and client intermediary we recognized the need to reflect user requirements in the design of the new version of the intranet. Rather than being a primarily summative report we recognized that our report would have to play a much more formative role. We structured our report as series of recommendations for three main areas: the development of the new version of the intranet; the definition of the intranet template; and strategic recommendations for CopperStone.

In our user advocate role we wanted to ensure that user needs were represented as fully as possible in the design of the new version of the intranet. We did this by ensuring that we provided recommendations that would be immediately useful to the developers (Orb). We produced a set of functional requirements listing organizational structures, access rights and specific features suggested by the users. We also included screen designs and menu structures.

At another level we wanted to ensure that user needs were also represented in future versions of this intranet as well as in intranets that might be developed for other local authorities. We did this by producing a second set of functional requirements for the intranet template to be developed by Orb. The major recommendation was that the template should support the community in implementing its own requirements.

We realized that we would also need to impress on CopperStone the need to take users into account and particularly to take account of the concerns of the local authority. We thus prepared a set of strategic recommendations advising CopperStone on the relationship it should adopt with system developers, particularly on how to ensure that the design of the system is user centred. It recommended how the introduction of such systems should be handled. Most importantly perhaps, it suggested how to manage the relationship with its client, the local authority.

Making a Successful Transition

The first step in making the transition from academic to real world evaluation is to be clear about the differences between the two contexts (see Table 1.1). Perhaps the major one is the emphasis in the commercial context on the product itself, unlike the academic where the product is often a means to an end. This shapes the techniques used and the form of results that are reported.

Another difference is the life-time of evaluation results. In the academic world the results are abstracted from and live on in the form of published

Table 1.1 Comparison of evaluation in the academic and commercial contexts

	Academic evaluation	Commercial evaluation
Objectives of project	Research aims are paramount. Main end goal is a new or novel theory that can be published.	Commercial aims are paramount. Main end goal is software product.
Role of evaluation	To test or refine a theory.	Often seen as a final validation.
Stage in the life cycle	Clearly defined at start of project.	Often done too late, or not aware of need for on-going evaluation.
Constraints	Appropriate time and budget for evaluation. Analysis allowed for.	Quick turn-around. Low budget (particularly for evaluation).
Subjects used	Willing or not "real".	Pressured. Difficult for consultant to access via the client.
Types of results gathered	May be narrow in scope or very detailed.	Must be concise.
How results are used	Abstracted and generalized into a theory.	Results must be specific to the product. Must be formative in order to have an impact.
Audience for results	Aimed at academic peers. Long-lived, beyond duration of project.	Aimed at developers or client. Relevant over lifetime of product.

papers. In a commercial context, once an evaluation report is completed, that is usually the end of things. A frustration of most consultants is not knowing what becomes of their results and recommendations (CopperStone being no exception). (In fact, this chapter is a rare opportunity to actually reflect on the process surrounding commercial work.)

Perhaps the biggest difference we noticed between the two contexts was the change in our roles. As academic evaluators we followed the fixed role of "objective" evaluator. In our case study we found ourselves constantly shifting and adopting new roles. We started by offering ourselves as evaluators. We then saw the need to define ourselves as conceptual designers. When talking to users we became requirements gatherers and user advocates. When dealing with our client's client we were cast in the most difficult role of all – intermediary.

The changes in situation and circumstances can be quite daunting at first. However, it is important to recognize that these are normal in real-world evaluation. The important thing is to be aware of the changes in situation and be clear on the role you choose to adopt. In this way your contribution can be defined in your own terms and remains under your control.

Lessons Learned

- Academic objectivity is a luxury that cannot be afforded in the politically sensitive commercial world. As an evaluator you may be called upon to adopt a variety of roles depending on the situation, and must be prepared to justify assuming these roles – or not.

- Be aware of the stage in the project life-cycle that you are being brought in at, the wider context of the work and the reasons behind the evaluation being commissioned.

- Even when an evaluation is seemingly summative it also needs to be formative, constructive and practical, to ensure that results are used and there is some impact on the product.

- You must know the agenda and stances of other stakeholders in the project in order to effectively manage your relationships with them.

No Usability Test Is an Island: Is Our Expertise Enough on Its Own?

2

Tim Westall

As technology products continue to offer more services to more types of user for more reasons, it's becoming harder and harder to make a living as an expert in only one area. When so many factors contribute to the way people respond to a web-site or a technology product, it seems increasingly that usability expertise is no longer enough in itself. Instead, experts in a number of specialities now need to know more about each other if they are to be able to give clients what they want. Branding, marketing, technology, consumer research and graphic design are mingling with each other and with usability to influence the way users experience technology – it's very difficult to apply one without an awareness of the other. This chapter illustrates the pitfalls of having too much as well as too little expertise, and argues for both a greater integration of skillsets and a deeper appreciation of expertise.

Introduction

These days, it's increasingly rare for a usability test to be just about usability. While there is a greater appreciation and awareness of usability testing, increasingly you may be finding that you're being asked to provide a usability service when the client (often without realizing it) needs something else entirely. Imagine a car manufacturer coming to you asking for help with the redesign of the dashboard, which he thinks will provide the solution to all his problems. In fact, he'd sell more cars if the model weren't so ugly, the engine was upgraded and somebody built some decent roads. To help him out, you'd need an appreciation of aesthetics, engineering and transport infra-structure on top of your core discipline of human factors.

We can see similar patterns emerging with usability. People ask for help on usability but actually need help with branding, customer research, marketing or relationship management. Sometimes they need help with them all! This chapter draws on a number of practical case studies where there were many other factors beyond "usability" in play. It points to how usability practitioners can continue to add value in their specialist area while being more aware of the broader context and blurring boundaries around them.

The Big Picture

The technology-led rush to market of most e-businesses was so chaotic that many simply forgot to pack the brand strategy, marketing plan and usability testing. Consequent under-performance combined with a dramatic change in investor sentiment has led to a new sense of realism. At a user level, this means a more pragmatic approach, intolerance of under-performance, polarising loyalty and an ever-declining list of primary bookmarks. At a business level, this means the challenge is now on to build the most attractive, efficient sites that people will find good enough to recommend to a friend. Usability has a big part to play.

There was a time in late 1999 when the web-site homepage was the defining icon for the new economy. We are now moving beyond that. For a start, the "old/new" division looks increasingly irrelevant. It's more the case that any business now has more ways to offer more services through more channels than ever before, be they selling socks or software.

Erstwhile pureplays such as Egg (an online bank) and amazon are now openly moving towards a high street presence. Although it hasn't happened yet, there is every indication that mobile (m-)commerce will grow exponentially over the next few years, and ye olde "homepage on a PC" will just be one of a number of ways of accessing a service. Usability will need to evolve beyond the hegemony of the PC, and the mobile device people certainly need some help with usability, judging by the first wave of Wireless Application Protocol (WAP) in particular.

From Rational "User" to Unreasonable, Demanding "Customer"

The language of usability testing betrays its roots. Aimed at IT professionals looking for efficient tools, usability grew up concerned with users who spent hours a day on a computer with a "professional" interest in the subject.

In the world of mainstream e-business, things couldn't be more different. It's about customers rather than users. The online experience is just one of many encounters the customer has with a brand or a business, and the web-site is often not the most important. And overall, customers are getting more demanding of service, less tolerant of under-delivery and more expecting of "good deals", so they can feel "smart". Business owners have educated people to think this way, through improving service dramatically and setting expectations ever higher. Within this context, many commercial web-sites are embarrassingly inept and very much the "weakest link".

Two years ago we were all surfing, happy to spend hours wandering around the Internet and exploring to our heart's content. When we found something interesting or useful, it was a nice surprise. Evolution of online behaviour has been rapid. As well as the surfers, many new user typologies are emerging:

- *Divers* know what they want and know how to find it. They crave information and mastery of the hidden depths of a subject. Typically, they'll have someone on their family with a medical condition their GP knows little about, so they'll be reading all the leading research in the area. They spend a lot of time online, love the Internet and keep coming up with gems

- *Quick dippers* know what they want and see the Internet as a means to an end. It's a practical tool, but they don't particularly enjoy for its own sake so look to minimise the time they spend online. When it comes to online shopping, if the phone or catalogue are faster or more reliable, they'll reject the Internet without a second thought.

- *Beach bums* are sociable types who really just want to chat with their mates. They'll spend ages online, but rarely venture beyond Hotmail. They're not prepared to pay for anything and cling to the original ethos of the Internet as a means of facilitating communication and understanding.

- *Lifeguards* might be parents or employers, and are increasingly worried about the dangers and temptations lurking beneath the surface. While they can see the value of the Internet for learning and communicating, they would like to see it much more tightly controlled (so only they will be able to find the way to hotbabes.com)

From WHAT to WHY

A lot of usability testing measures the wrong things. The true measures of success, as with any brand, are how many customers you have, how often they visit, how much they buy and how likely they are to recommend you to a friend. This demands better quantitative measurement and smarter combinations of qualitative depth techniques to understand not just *what* people are doing, but also *why* they are doing it. Internet user research still has a long way to evolve, much of it still being locked in the spurious quantitative comfort zone of screen-tracking statistics.

The benefits of greater speed, choice and value are well on the way to becoming Internet generic benefits. Likewise, sites are expected to be fast, easy to navigate and intuitive. As mentioned earlier, customer expectations are rising steadily, increasing pressure to deliver distinctive, branded experiences that give people a reason to choose one site over another and repeatedly come back for more. To date, much online "branding" has actually been an obstacle (slow download times, gratuitous graphics) and the challenge is now to simplify online offers and integrate them with the rest of the brand experience.

Some Practical Illustrations

The following examples are drawn from projects we have worked on over the past 18 months. Things are kept deliberately anonymous because they are not all great success stories. However, they do all illustrate that, although a usability test was the original requirement, significant other dimensions needed considering.

Don't Bank on It . . .

A high street bank was looking to set up an online offer targeted at mainstream retail customers. Their motivation was to reduce "cost to serve", where the cost of an Internet transaction was estimated to be 0.1p, against 10p on the phone and £1.20 in a branch. In developing a web-site, they wanted to stress the benefits of speed and cost reduction, and to position the web-site as a standalone channel that looked and felt different to the rest of the brand.

Qualitative research showed that the real benefit was actually to do with how it made customers feel about dealing with the bank. Whereas in-branch, the "parent–child" relationship made people feel uneasy and resentful, on-line customers felt much more on a level with the bank, where they had some influence and control. What the online offer did was to transform the relationship to an "adult–adult" one, increasing people's confidence and encouraging them to do more things with the bank.

Another critical insight was that the vast majority of people did not consider the web-site as anything other than a new way of dealing with something they were already familiar with and trusting of. In other words, they saw it as a smart new channel that they would dip into as well as continuing to deal with the bank in other ways. By trying to force people to choose one channel over another ("are you a web person or a phone person?") the bank could have made a big mistake.

In terms of usability and site design, this thinking followed through to a site that concentrated on doing few things but doing them well, and avoiding cross-selling brochureware that just got in the way.

The Power of a Brand . . .

A leading package-holiday company was looking to develop an online travel agency. Already, over 2,000 online travel agents existed so theirs would need to really stand out. Because of their size and stature, the company had access to the widest range of holidays at the best prices, a position that many claim but only they could deliver.

A site was designed and was subject to intense usability testing until everyone was satisfied with it. The new orthodoxy of Jacob Nielsen minimalism and "best practice" had been enthusiastically adopted. An aggressive promotional plan was then put together and the team thought that it was onto a winner: a great site with "category killing" content behind it, plus the support of a big company to get things off the ground.

However, when it came to branding, the company decided to avoid their high street brand name, instead opting for a generic, indistinct dotcom label. Despite heavy marketing support, people didn't notice or remember the new brand, and visitors were 2 per cent of numbers forecast. Further usability work was commissioned, but little could be done to improve the ratings already achieved. So what was the problem?

Meanwhile, in another part of the same group of companies, somebody independently decided to slap the high street brand name onto a fairly primitive online travel agency that had been picked up by chance as part of a larger acquisition. Within a month, this rather clunky site had exceeded the business of the other (superior) offer 20-fold. What became apparent was that consumers were actively looking for established travel brands online, and were actively avoiding "cheap, cheap, cheap" pureplays. They simply didn't trust them, likening them to dodgy discount "bucketshops". Instead, they were quite happy to pay a small perceived premium in return for the confidence and trust of an established brand.

Shunting Offline Content Online

A leading national publishing group was going electronic. They could see the threat and the opportunity that the Internet represented and were eager to move their content online. Because they had a thriving local newspaper business, and because they could see the "make it local" power of the Internet, they decided to digitize their local newspaper business, leading on local news content. However, visitors to the sites were few and far between. Why? – they were known brands just operating via a new medium. Surely it must be a problem with usability – so a usability test and site redesign work was commissioned.

A little bit of thought and little bit of original research came up with two insights. First, and most fundamentally, the reasons people go to an online local news site are not the same as those for a real newspaper. Newspapers are browsed by those with time to browse, looking for information about things they/their friends are interested in. By contrast, online news-sites are visited by busy people seeking time-critical information. The second insight was that much of the online space the publishing group was seeking to compete in had already been taken. There are already established news sites, travel sites and weather sites that busy, time-critical information seekers have found and are very happy with

The unpalatable conclusion was that the whole thing was (a) too late onto the market; and (b) not aligned with the way people think and what they expect to find on arriving at a "local news" site. PS: This was not an acceptable conclusion and further site redesign and usability testing has been requested.

Keep It Simple, Stupid

A well-funded and heavily advertised online job/career site was looking to accelerate its growth. A cute brand identity had been created that was appealing and relevant to the younger end of the market and the early signs were reasonably encouraging. However, many competitive sites were now coming online, so it was felt very important to improve and differentiate the site ahead of competitors.

The new site had been devised with many new features, and the owners wanted it usability tested. They were aiming to appeal to an older target market, capturing more middle/senior managers through a higher level of jobs and numerous features/links aimed at establishing online communities around particular professions. The usability testers had two concerns.

The first involved the stimulus material. Highly designed "mock-up" pages of the proposed new site had been commissioned, with the aim of trying to bring the new vision for the site alive. This proved to be a misjudgement – the site looked so "finished" that all people could do was to criticize and judge it. After two disastrous consumer sessions, the stimulus material was changed to much rougher sketches that looked unfinished and thus invited respondents to "join the dots" and suggest many improvements.

As an aside, the need for realistic stimulus material in much online concept testing seems to be diminishing. With increasing online experience, people are more and more able to precisely describe their experience and stipulate their requirements of a site without having to go near a PC. In a way, it's somewhat like early advertising research, when the only way to test an idea was to actually film it first and then see if anybody liked it. These days of course, the audience has become so sophisticated that the roughest sketches of an advertising idea will usually suffice.

The second concern was to do with the broader context of job seeking and career development. As well as there being many online alternatives, the offline elements (i.e. recruitment agents, personal contacts, job ads pages) remain incredibly important. Therefore the testers wanted to spend some time exploring this broader context before diving into the detail of this particular site and its performance.

It turned out that the consumer expectations of the site were very clear indeed. They sought immediacy (more up to date than trade journals and newspapers, and no more than four clicks to find "a job for me"), anonymity (feel okay to browse, even if not actively searching) and comprehensiveness (full range expected). None of the four online brand leaders were delivering against these expectations. So, the message was simple: forget enhancements and "competitive differentiation" – just get the basics right. A simple conclusion, but a rather worrying one for online job sites as a whole.

Wrap Up Warm and Don't Catch Portalitis

As many business-to-business (B2B) and business-to-consumer (B2C) sectors begin to consolidate, everybody wants to be a portal – "the only place you'll ever to need to go for anything, ever" – capturing maximum potential market space in the process. A usability brief from a B2C clothing e-tailer asked if adding e-mail, chat rooms, loyalty points and a news channel would be a good idea. The idea was to create "stickiness", giving users more and more reasons to come back regularly to the site. Usability research with regular customers revealed that all of these proposed new features would offer some additional benefit. So the new site was launched and the number of visitors promptly fell. How could that be?

Subsequent detective work revealed that, when looked at overall, the combination of clothing, news, e-mail, chat and a (new online only) loyalty scheme was very confusing indeed. Going back to the car analogy, the usability team had been asked to check out the dashboard makeover when the car had actually had a fish-and-chip shop installed in the boot (that's how much sense it made to people). Usability was being used to justify "directionless enhancement", an all-too-common phenomenon in a technology-led business. One only needs to think of over-engineered digital camcorders and gadget-infested Japanese cars – they do have some appeal, but only to a small niche of middle-aged men that first need prising out of their garden sheds – or these days, their Internet dens.

A well-funded B2B portal start-up had conceived of the idea of a horizontal e-procurement and settlement portal. The concept had been well-researched and was found to be very appealing to a certain tranche of medium-sized businesses. However, the technology to deliver this was some way off, but there was great pressure from investors to get at least something up and running. An invidious "usability" brief was issued. After usability testing had showed that loads of links to other business information sites was desirable to users, and that the site was attractive, intuitive, etc., it was launched. The site was, in essence, a "coming soon" placard with a load of tenuous links to stronger sites around the edges. When hundreds of disappointed visitors began to complain, the usability team got a kicking. They had given the site a clean bill of health after all. If the usability team had had the courage to ask some bigger questions it could have been a different story.

Ways Forward for Usability

To remain relevant and influential, what should usability practitioners be doing? Consider the transition that market research departments are going through in established fmcg businesses. They are making the move from being responsive "customer score keepers" through to being expert research advisers to management, adding a broader business perspective above and beyond the technicalities of their own discipline.

Many have felt threatened by this transition, feeling that they are required to possess skills and knowledge it would take years to acquire properly. But the point is not to become an instant polymath, rather it's about taking a broader perspective and asking the right questions.

When it comes to usability testing of a web-site, we have found the following checklist very helpful;

1. Who is the site for?

   - How do you describe them?

   - What is your critical insight into their needs/attitudes/behaviours?

   - What will be their state of mind and what will they be expecting to find when they get to the site?

2. What is the site for?

   - What does it do for people? (is this clearly communicated?)

   - What do you want people to do / pay for?

   - How do you want people to think and feel having used the site?

3. What is the context?

   - How will people be made aware of the site?

   - How important is the site in the context of the overall offer (other channels)?

   - What is better and different about this site compared to alternatives (on and offline)?

While it's a straightforward list of questions, getting to the answers is becoming harder and harder. Web-sites are increasingly serving a huge diversity of people who visit for a great variety of reasons. If you're developing a site, you need to be able to understand and respond to this complexity, drawing on a very wide range of complementary skills. You need to be able to recognise what it is people are really asking for and broadening your response. On one level, you need to be able to pull out the range of needs which might exist and direct people towards, for example, brand experts, marketing experts, or Customer Relationship Management experts. At another level, you need to be clear about where usability analysis can contribute something useful.

Only Time Will Tell . . .

Gazing momentarily into our crystal ball, what might happen to purveyors of usability testing, web-site design, marketing, research, and branding in the near future? We can see the beginnings of two potential scenarios;

In the first scenario, we move from thousands of flaky dotcoms down to a few dozen big players, most of whom are integrated clicks and bricks. Their owners establish a dominant market position and begin to internalise a lot of the expertise they need, recruiting a usability specialist, a branded marketing specialist, a CRM (Customer Relationship Management) specialist and a web-site designer. These experts then draw on support from specialist outside agencies when they need to. So usability experts become more specialised, either as "buyers" within a corporation, or "sellers" within a specialist agency.

In the second scenario, the richness and complexity of e-business as it evolves means that the narrow perspective of any specialist becomes increasingly unsatisfactory. A new breed of e-business generalist emerges, with experience in at least a couple of areas. Specialist knowledge is still very important, but tends to reside within larger, generalist consultancies. Many claim to do this today, but in reality are little more than rebadged software sales machines that lack credibility and critical mass in anything beyond technology or graphic design.

We can see aspects of both scenarios unfolding today. Arguably, e-business is still so immature that specialist areas need to evolve in their own right before they can be assimilated into something bigger. So it might be that scenario 1 evolves into scenario 2, but probably at a faster pace than we have seen before. Whatever happens, usability folk will need to have an increasing appreciation for other areas, while at the same time becoming more expert in their own.

Lessons Learned

- Sometimes you need to dig beneath the surface to understand the real user benefit of an online service.

- In some cases, recognize that online is really no more than "another way" to access services people are already using.

- Strong brands take years and millions of pounds to create. If your client has one, try to exploit it somehow.

- When it comes to consumers spending hundreds of pounds online, trust in an established brand is a crucial enabler.

- Don't assume a successful offline concept will succeed online without a rethink.

- Understand what people might expect when they get to a site, and what their frame of reference will be (alternatives they will compare your site to).

- Consumers can help you develop a site if you have the right approach and loose stimulus material.

- In the quest for competitive edge, don't lose sight of the basics.

- Challenge the brief!

- If a site is suffering from portalitis, so its' purpose isn't clear to you, the eventual intended user won't stand a chance.

Who Moved My Lab?: The Effect of Constant Organizational Change on Usability Practice

3

Jose Coronado

Competitive pressure has forced organizations of all kinds to become more flexible in their structure and more responsive to market changes. Mergers and acquisitions are commonplace, often followed by redundancy programmes. While this may make for a reduced cost base, constant organizational change can have a potentially adverse impact on groups within the organization and the way they work. Usability engineers are no exception and must react to changes in the operational model or in management, often needing to modify methodologies quickly and effectively. This chapter covers three major organizational events in a large business software company. It provides details of the challenges presented by these events, shows how usability professionals responded to these changes, and describes the lessons the team learned in the process.

Introduction

Growing software organizations often face repeated dramatic changes in their operational structures. Either because of a company acquisition, or simply because a product line expands, companies change and adapt their product development processes to meet the demands imposed by these changes. Different business models and product development philosophies can have a marked effect on the approach to and execution of usability activities. In addition, organizational changes can strengthen or undermine the role and the effectiveness that usability engineering has in the company's product development process.

At Hyperion Solutions Corporation, three major organizational events over the last few years have had a strong impact on the practice of usability. This chapter describes the details of the political atmosphere when the changes occurred and how the usability professionals reacted to those challenges. The first event describes how the practice of user interface design and usability evolved from an informal group of individuals into an organized and structured usability team. The group's formation enhanced usability's status throughout the company. The second event describes the process of a merger between Hyperion and another company both of which had different product development philosophies and how that merger affected individual members of the usability team as well as the methods and processes used. The last event explains what happened when the product development organization was decentralised into business units and how it affected the usability practitioners.

The Organization: Hyperion Solutions

Hyperion Solutions Corporation develops and markets analytic application software to more than 4,000 customer companies worldwide. In 1994, an informal group of four engineers, including the author, introduced usability methods to the company as Hyperion was embarking on its second major Windows-GUI based product. At that time, Hyperion was actively localizing its software for use by its international user base and this group assumed the responsibility for user interface design and usability activities. Before this transition, each was a member of a different product development team dealing with programming, documentation, quality assurance and visual design. As an ad hoc usability team, the engineers decided to assume additional responsibilities, to include overseeing user interface consistency among the products, and to incorporate User Interface (UI) recommendations relative to software internationalization.

Despite having to make time outside normal working hours to meet, this ad hoc group set in place user interface and localization standards. Activities included requirements gathering, convening focus groups, prototyping of UI designs and product usability evaluation testing (Rubin, 1994). However, given its casual nature, individual efforts had little impact on the projects. The software developers in the project teams did not always implement many of the recommendations, and it was hard to make the project managers allocate time for usability activities in the product development plan. Up to this point, the UI design was the sole developer's responsibility. Project managers perceived UI design iterations and usability evaluations as time-consuming activities that extended the overall product development process. Furthermore, no executive support or management direction of usability existed, making the work of these four (UI) engineers very difficult within the organization. They did not belong to any Human Factors or User-Centred Design Group; each reported to a different project manager and each was part of a product team.

At this early stage, usability did not have any visibility in the development organization. Usability activities persisted in this unfavourable environment only because UI engineers believed in it and made concerted efforts to maintain visibility.

From Ad Hoc to Added Value: the Formation of the User-Centred Design (UCD) Group

One of the key factors that influenced the successful formation of the User-centred Design (UCD) Group at Hyperion was executive support. The senior vice-president of Product Development had raised questions about the product development process as it related to the users' involvement. This executive knew that the success of a product development process needed the participation of the users early. Believing that a successful product was not designed in a box, the senior vice-president (SVP) provided the necessary executive support. This coincided with an attempt by the ad hoc group to justify the formation of a centralized UCD Group. Simultaneously, during the preparation of a proposal for a usability group at the bottom of the organization, the senior executive, at the top, was raising questions as to why this group did not exist in the company.

In September 1997, the UCD Group was officially chartered as part of the central development organization, reporting directly to the SVP of Development (*Fig. 3.1*). Three senior UI engineers and one senior visual designer comprised this group, including the author. A Senior Manager assigned to manage this group set tangible goals and management directions. In less than 6 months, the group doubled its size, adding one usability engineer and three more UI engineers. By the end of 1998, the group had 13 engineers distributed across the product development sites located in the US (California, Florida and Connecticut) and Canada.

The successful beginning of the group was not gratuitous. We were expected to demonstrate the value of activities such as task analysis and product usability evaluation; it was not enough just to put a check mark on the activity as it took place. The different stakeholders looked for specific

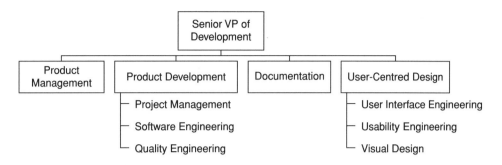

Figure 3.1 Development organization – Fall 1997

information as the outcome. For example, when I conducted a task analysis (Hackos and Redish, 1998) session for one of our financial products, I gained a clear understanding of the business process our product was supporting. However, that was not enough benefit to the product team. The product manager looked for information to help validate or gather new information about product requirements. At the same time, the development manger looked for product enhancements that could be implemented in the short term. As a usability engineer, it was my responsibility to respond to these expectations, facilitate the information gathering process and report the findings in a clear and concise manner.

Moreover, as a group, we needed to collect success stories of our involvement in the different projects. For example, results from usability evaluation sessions that helped us ensure that changes in the UI were incorporated. When we gathered positive feedback from a client or partner about the ease-of-use of a product, or when a market analyst criticized our product's UI, we were able to make the people in the development teams listen. In addition, anecdotes with developers, implementation of design recommendations, and successful project conclusions helped us build a library of projects that we could showcase. We made sure to inform other development teams and different areas of the organization about these stories.

Additionally, the UCD manager helped us by providing guidance and negotiating our involvement with the product development teams. Even though the group doubled its size in less than a year, we still had limited resources and were not able to support every single project under development. The manager chose the ones that would have more visibility assessing the potential number of users (i.e. web reporting versus an administration module), the development time allocated to the project, the revenue expectation and how the product aligned with the overall company direction and strategy.

By doing this, the impact and the exposure that we had as usability professionals, was even greater.

The philosophy of a senior executive aligned well with the beliefs of a handful of engineers. The positive chemistry of this match allowed the usability practice to take off. The role of usability engineering in the development process was strengthened by the support of a centralized UCD group. This attracted many new usability professionals to the group. However, we got comfortable with the executive support. We did not see the need to evolve the marketing strategy for usability services because upper management sometimes forced our involvement in projects. We tried very hard to drive the development process towards a user-centred design process, and we lost sight of the need to be flexible in our methods and processes. Different teams and different products require distinct approaches, and we had to adapt our activities and methodologies to them; instead of having them modify their development process to accommodate us. The constant growth of the company and the demands imposed by a merger would present new challenges to this team.

When Philosophies Collide: the Merger of Two Companies

A merger or acquisition has a serious impact at every level of an organization, and product development is no exception. In this case, the two merging development groups had distinct product development philosophies. One group lacked general awareness of the benefits and risks associated with the use of usability engineering methodologies. In addition, the characteristics of the products developed in each pre-merger company were quite different. One development team produced open technology software that enabled companies to build applications with it, while the other team mainly produced closed packaged software applications. Several perception problems associated with usability activities existed: some argued that these activities would cause a project to extend or delay its release cycles, while others did not see a benefit associated with integrating usability into the development process of certain products. In addition, the lack of communication between the different development sites was a key stumbling block that hindered the product development process and presented a roadblock to reach consistent UI design across the different products.

In the Fall of 1998, Hyperion Software merged with Arbor Software, an OLAP database technology developer. This merger formed what is known today as

Hyperion Solutions. Predictably, the product roadmap of the new company changed, since the development organization faced the challenge of providing integrated products. These new products needed to meet users' needs and expectations in a very compressed development cycle. The traditional product development process (*Fig. 3.2*) suggests that one third of the project time had to be dedicated to perform up-front work on requirements gathering, understanding the business process and designing the UI to support it, while two thirds had to be dedicated to implementation and quality.

The two pre-merger development organizations will be regarded as Group A and Group B. The development process philosophy of Group A did not include usability in its product development cycle at all and focused more on user interface design. This group did not have any Human Factors or Usability engineers in its staff, and no user feedback was integrated until late in the beta cycle. At this point only product bugs were fixed, but there was not enough time or resources to undertake any major user interface design changes that were needed.

In contrast, Group B had been working with UI engineers for a few years. However, some resistance from software developers and project managers to fully integrate usability in the product development cycle still existed. Overall, this development group supported the usability work with varying levels of enthusiasm.

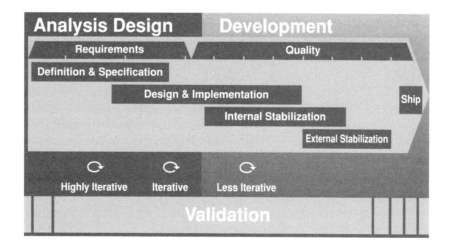

Figure 3.2 High level overview of the traditional product development process

These colliding philosophies caused conflicts between the software developers from Group A and the UI engineers. Immediately, each regarded the other as an outsider and contrasting design methodologies and recommendations encountered much resistance. The developers complained that their creativity was being stifled; their argument was that one of the most interesting and fun aspects of programming, the UI, was being taken away from them. Software developers were also sceptical about the direct benefits that involving users in requirement validation or product usability evaluation activities would have in the product.

Moreover, the release cycles differed dramatically between the two groups. Group A would have a major release every 6 months or so, minor releases every 3 months, and a patch release every month. In contrast, Group B would have one major release per year, and minor releases and patches only as it deemed necessary. However, Group's A rapid software development process was a manageable challenge because of its different usability methods that could be used for faster development cycles. Instead of full-scale usability sessions, Group A could quickly prepare paper or semi-interactive prototypes to gather feedback. Internal participants from other areas like support and client services were brought in for quick and dirty usability sessions, and when it was not possible to run these sessions because of time constraints, a heuristic review (Nielsen and Mack, 1994) was carried out with other UI engineers using storyboards, smoke screen prototypes or just the current development version.

Perceptions of Usability Benefits Can Vary

Neither Group A nor Group B was fully aware of the benefits of usability. Every project required strategic meetings with development, product and marketing managers, and even though it was not necessary to make a business case for every project in terms of the funding, both groups needed to sell the value of the service constantly, reiterating what benefits usability activities would bring to each project. UI engineers needed to make a business case for time and have the project managers include these activities in the project plan not only as milestones, but also to allocate time to address findings and use the information gathered.

The development teams were not the only ones at fault when it came to understanding the benefits of usability. Adding to the problems the usability team already faced within the organization was the awkward way the UCD group marketed the service. UCD engineers and sometimes the UCD manager would focus more on the details of how to plan and conduct an activity like a usability evaluation session, rather than on the benefits that such activity would have in the product and the development team.

To overcome this problem and to highlight the benefits behind usability methods, UCD organized brown bag lunches and usability awareness sessions for product development teams including managers, quality assurance, documentation, and software development. Additionally, members of the UCD group developed one-, two- and three-day GUI (Graphical User Interface) and web design courses. We developed some of these training sessions independently and some in collaboration with a consulting firm specialized in human factors. We showcased GUI industry standards, corporate GUI guidelines, as well as practical data collection methods. The objectives of these sessions and courses were two-fold: first, to educate the members of the development team about GUI design best practices; and second, to force them to think and question the potential impact that implementation decisions would have on the end user interaction. Overall, these courses and awareness sessions were successful because the developers started looking towards the UCD Group for guidance and feedback during the development process.

That Old Chestnut: "but Usability Testing Delays the Product Development Process"

A common obstacle for usability engineering includes the belief that UI design iterations or product usability evaluations add time to the development process and delay the projects. This probably still is one of the most difficult arguments to overcome. As explained previously, the cycles managed by Group B were more favourable to incorporate usability simply because the time frames in the development process were wider. In contrast, the process employed by Group A handled shorter periods between releases.

One of my colleagues was involved in the UI design for two integration products involving developers from Group A and B. The objective of this project was to design one interaction model that could be used in both products. Throughout the design stage, my colleague held design meetings that involved Product Management, Development and Documentation.

Everybody was aware of what direction the design was taking, had the chance to provide input, and as a team, identified potential implementation restrictions early. The developers started working in the back end integration aspects, while the design was tested with users. At the end, when the UI model was handed off, the developers mentioned that the up-front analysis and design work saved them time in the implementation stage. This project was a success story not only for the UCD team, but also for the newly centralised development organization.

Communication Problems Between Sites and Teams

Ineffective communication between development sites further hindered usability work. Both Group A and Group B had development teams in the East Coast and in the West Coast, distributed at four different sites. The UCD group did not have UI engineers in all sites, so we had limited exposure and team interaction in some geographical locations. Some times, the communications within each development group were limited. The level of expertise and specialisation required by some products isolated project teams. To alleviate this problem, UCD engineers were forced to set up cross-product management meetings to discuss issues that directly impacted more than one product. If these meetings were not possible, we made sure to include short presentations of relevant design activities of other products during the regular status meetings of our own projects.

The work of the usability engineers was highly regarded in those product development teams where UCD had demonstrated the value of its involve-ment. Product and development managers encouraged developers to work with us during the design process. Since we were not part of a specific product team, we had the chance to see several projects simultaneously. We were able to build the bridge to overcome the communications gap between teams. At the same time, we provided input in the development process that enabled the teams to reach a more consistent UI across the different products. However, since we did not have UCD representatives in each geographical site, the communication and UI consistency efforts did not cover the entire organization.

The year following the merger was very tough for the usability engineers: differences in development philosophies and beliefs were hard to reconcile and resistance in the development teams to integrate usability practices remained. The work continued to come to the group from those teams that believed in the value of usability. However, this would not be the last major organizational change that the usability team would have to fight through.

A New Operational Model

Early in the Spring of 2000, the business model of the company changed from a centralised product development group (*Fig. 3.2*) into a business unit – cost centre model (*Fig. 3.3*). The development organization was decentral-ized into five distinct Business Units distributed across six development sites. These business units integrated areas like Product Marketing and UI

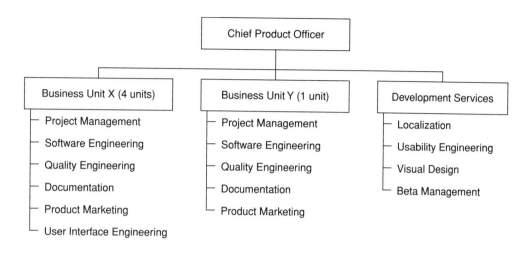

Figure 3.3 Partial snapshot of the Product Development Organization, Fall, 2000

Engineering into their organization. Each business unit was responsible for the development of a specific line of Hyperion's product suite that covered more than 20 products. In addition, Development Services was created as a cost centre grouping several shared services. Areas such as Usability Engineering, Localization, Beta Management, and Visual Design were situated in this new group.

Divided We Fall? Splitting of the UI Engineering Resources Across the Business Units

The business units took on the focus of UI design efforts, while the cost centre services group became responsible for data collection and validation efforts. Once again, we needed to build business cases for usability engineering activities, especially for those business units where there were no or limited user interface engineering resources.

One of the most recent projects in which the usability team was involved included a task analysis activity for a next generation product. The current product offering has a strong feature set. However, evolving technology and new system architecture requirements made this project an important initiative to the business unit. The task analysis objectives and benefits were discussed with the product development team including the product, project and development managers, and the UI engineer. Even though we had the support from the team to conduct this activity, there was still some scepticism about the benefits that would derive from it. By including a cross sample of participants like subject experts, partners, current clients and prospects, we were able to collect valuable information that was going to be used by the different stakeholders. The product and development managers received the information about product requirements and enhancements very well. At the same time, the UI engineer collected detailed information about the different business processes that could then be translated into UI design alternatives. Selling the benefit and the value of the data collection activity was not easy. However, through teamwork and constant communication with the product team members, usability engineering was able to bring this project to a successful conclusion.

This new business unit/cost centre model forced usability engineering to partner with the business units and align the strategic objectives (Kaplan and Norton, 2001) of the UI design and data collection activities with the objectives of the product development team. The main goal for both groups is to provide the best application on the deadline. As illustrated in the previous example, when working properly, there is little friction between them, and at the end everybody wins. The business unit has a great product, and the usability engineer has another successful project to add to the portfolio.

Changes in Executive Support

Varying support is probably a constant that all usability practitioners face at one time or another. The support for our activities changes when people come or leave the teams that we interact with. In Hyperion's case, the dramatic transformation in the business operational model forced several personnel changes. With the business unit – cost centre model, the support of one key executive for usability activities was no longer enough. Now the general manager (GM) had the autonomy and control over every operational aspect of the business unit. In addition, the GM was now accountable for handling corporate strategic objectives such as time to market and high customer satisfaction, which clearly presented challenges to the practice of usability. In each business unit, the UI and usability engineers needed to secure support at different levels of the development team in order to be successful. Executive support at the top of the business unit was important, but it was not necessarily the most effective. Buy-in at the mid-level management layer and at the developer level were key to move UI design initiatives and usability activities forward.

New Organization, New Marketing Strategy

The usability engineer became a consultant to the business unit. This forced all of us in the usability group to clearly redefine the portfolio of services. These services had to cover all data collection efforts such as task analysis and usability evaluation sessions as well as web and GUI design and training. The arguments used for marketing these services concentrated on the business benefits derived from usability engineering activities and the risks associated with leaving users out of the development process. Usability Engineers needed to make different emphasis when addressing different audiences. For example, Sales and Consulting required an emphasis on how usability activities would help increase revenue while Development would expect to see information related to shortening delivery times. Besides the benefit information presented at the executive management level, for the project managers and the rest of the development team, additional details were added. We mapped activities according to the time frames presented in the product development cycle (*Fig. 3.4*) and also mentioned the deliverables from each activity.

In Hyperion's case, one positive aspect in this business unit/cost centre operational model dealt with funding. As part of Development Services, usability engineering was fully funded. As a consequence, usability consulting services could be positioned as a free resource available to the business units. Upper management in the business unit did not have to make a decision about economic resources because they did not need to pay for usability services.

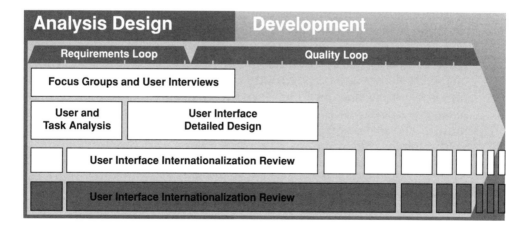

Figure 3.4 Usability activities mapped within the development process

The continued centralization of usability and visual design allowed for professional specialisation and uniformity of certain visual elements across products. Consistent usability methodologies and evaluations are essential across different projects. This also allowed for facilities like the usability labs to expand and be used on a regular basis by the different product teams. The UI engineers understood the usability engineers and visual designers much better than the developers or project managers did. Through close collaboration between the former members of the UCD group, the business units were able to employ Usability and Visual Design services in a more effective and appropriate manner.

Even though the UCD group was decentralised following the business unit/cost centre model, the practice of usability continued. Constant collaboration between the UI and usability engineers enabled data collection activities to take place. The apparent weakened position of independent professional disciplines was dissipated by the continuous support at different levels of the organization. The company's commitment to provide products with higher user quality experience is reflected in the corporate strategy. The UI and Usability practitioners have faced challenging situations, but at the end, they have found support among themselves, from peers, and even from clients who feel great about having the chance to participate in the product development process.

Conclusion

The operational structure at Hyperion continues to evolve. At the time of writing, Usability Engineering along with the other groups in Development Services, is being aligned with the Chief Technology Officer organization. This change is supposed to strengthen the perception of usability as a technologic and scientific oriented field. Nevertheless, the ties with the UI engineers across the business units need to remain solid. Close collaboration is required in order to achieve the common goal of providing the best quality products within the time frames and budgets defined for each project. These changes also make the usability practitioners develop flexible methodologies for different situations, teams and products. Some professionals resist or disagree with the changes and move on. For those who have faced the challenges, the reward of being able to contribute to the development of successful products has paid off.

Lessons Learned

Major organizational events can have a profound influence on usability practice, but when usability professionals respond positively to the challenges and changes presented by these events, productivity and support remain high. Here are the most important lessons the usability team learned in the process.

- Choose your battles. Weigh and compare projects assessing the potential number of end-users reached, the development time allocated to the project, the revenue expectation and how the product aligns with the overall company direction and strategy. Put people on high priority, high visibility projects.

- Be prepared to be flexible, as established methods may need to be adapted to specific situations. Time is essential in rapid application development environments and the development teams expect quick turnaround from the usability engineering methods you employ.

- Do not take executive support for granted, since organizations evolve and people move on. Executive support is essential to get usability activities started; however, at the end you have to work with the developers who are in charge of directly implementing your design ideas or enhancements. Regardless of how much upper management support you have, you need the developers to buy in. This will increase your chances to positively impact the projects in which you are involved.

- Integrate and work closely with the development team. Do not be afraid to share the ownership of design ideas. A participatory approach will make your life easier and increase the potential influence that you can have in the interaction and interface design of the product.

- Be aware of technology trends, marketing expectations and internationalization requirements. Multidisciplinary collaboration and continual communication with Development, Marketing and Localization departments will help usability engineering be more effective.

References

Hackos J, Redish J (1998) User and Task Analysis for Interface Design. John Wiley & Sons, Inc New York

Kaplan R, Norton D (2001) Strategy Focused Organizations: How Balanced Scorecard Companies Thrive in the New Business Environment. Harvard Business School Press, Boston, MA

Nielsen J, Mack R. (1994) Usability Inspection Methods. John Wiley & Sons, Inc., New York

Rubin J (1994) Handbook of Usability Testing: How to Plan, Design, and Conduct Effective Usability Tests. John Wiley & Sons, Inc New York

"What Does That Button Do?" Effective Project Scheduling Around Complicated and Unfamiliar Technology

4

Avi Parush

This chapter describes the experience of a usability consultancy hired by a small start-up developing Wireless Application Protocol (WAP)-based system. Desinging the user interface for a cellular Internet system under a very tight time-to-market schedule is still a new challenge for usability professionals, and in this case, both the developers and the usability consultants lacked previous experience with the new technology. Consequently, the developers had a hard time defining the requirements well in advance, and the usability professionals lacked proper design methodologies.

The need to develop a design methodology and an alarming increase in the number of design iterations because of changing requirements took a significant chunk from the already lean schedule. While the usability consultants perceived the delays to be insignificant with little impact on the delivery schedule, the developers' perception was of serious delays in getting what they needed. The lessons learned from this case are relevant to projects where a new and unfamiliar technology is introduced. Project tasks such as requirements definition and the possible need to develop new design methodologies should be taken into account in the scheduling. In addition, consultants must remain open to warning signs that different groups have widely differing perceptions and expectations of the process, in order to prevent these materializing into real problems. More personal communication between the developer and the consultant can play a critical role to bring perceptions to the surface.

Background

The Internet porting to a variety of platforms is becoming pervasive. Particularly attractive is the possibility of providing the end user with Internet accessibility "on-the-go" via mobile devices such as the cellular phone and the Personal Digital Assistant (PDA). The mobile Internet introduced new challenges to usability experts, not only in terms of the professional aspects but also in terms of the "behind the scenes" dynamics of the development process. The case described here involves a small development start-up company that commisioned usability consultants to design the user interface of a cellular Internet system. This chapter focuses on the scheduling aspects and the various human and technological factors that affected it.

Project Objectives and Definitions

The original definition included the following statement of work: design the user interface of the WAP-based cellular phone, the web-site, and the interface of the Short Messages System (SMS) mechanism. Priority was placed on the interface of the WAP-based part. The planned work followed the conventional user interface design framework of first designing the concept, then prototyping the general architecture of the work flow and major screens, and finally proceeding to the detailed design of each screen and each interaction.

Team Structure

The user interface design team was originally composed of two members, the project leader who was the primary responsible person for the work, and an additional team member whose intended job was to assist the project leader in specific tasks. This additional team member would accompany the project leader throughout the entire process. From the developer's side, a project coordinator was assigned to be the primary liaison with the user interface consultants. The role of that liaison person was to

- Convey the technical and functional specifications of the product to the designers.

- Be an active partner in making user-centred decisions which were critical for the user interface design framework.

- Monitor and approve the progress of the work, primarily in terms of the deliverables from the design consultants.

Initial Scheduling

The initial scheduling was based on the perception that this is "just another user interface design project". Following the conventional design framework, separate times were allotted for the conceptual design and the detailed design phase. The conceptual phase included a learning period during which the user interface designers (using user-centred design methodologies) were supposed to have learned and analysed the functional requirements of the system. In addition, the learning included understanding the technological aspects. Based on those assumptions, six weeks was scheduled for the conceptual design work and three months for the detailed design phase of the WAP-based cellular phone and SMS interface.

Methodological Issues

The major problem plaguing this project was the developer's claims that the design work was often behind schedule. Two methodological issues played a role in getting the "schedule snowball" rolling. The first were the conceptual versus detailed design differences between between a conventional user interface and a WAP-based interface. The second issue was the methodical tools required as a result of that difference.

Conceptual Versus Detailed Design

The conventional user interface design framework needed to be modified and tailored to the unique characteristics of designing a WAP-based user interface. Conventional conceptual design deals with the following:

1. The overall organization of the user interface components to ensure they represent the subject matter of the application and the functional requirements.

2. The navigation policy that enables the completion of all intended workflows and user tasks.

3. The determination of the general look and feel of the user interface.

The conventional detailed design phase is actually the allocation of all the functional details of the application into this structure. This includes all the actions and parameters that the user will need to activate, view, create, and modify, or any other possible interaction. This conventional approach turned out to be less appropriate for a WAP-based user interface. The core of the problem is that there is very little, or almost no, distinction between the conceptual and the detailed design phases in cellular Internet. When designing the interface structure, it's necessary to design the details of many screens since their content actually lists options for branching to other screens. The implications of this methodological difference is that the required time for the conceptual phase is significantly shorter than what is required in conventional user interface design, and conversely, the time for detailed design is significantly longer.

Tools

Since the conceptual structure of the user interface significantly overlaps the detailed design of many screens, there was an immediate need for appropriate design tools. In particular, a tool for rapid structuring of a screen tree structure was needed urgently. Such a tool had to have the following features:

1. Enable the creation of a screen tree structure;

2. Change and edit it frequently;

3. Communicate the structure and show the details of many screens.

While such tools seem to be in abundance, the combination of the need to show the overall structure, on the one hand, and yet show details of the screens, on the other hand, was lacking from many conventional tools. This need is not often present in conventional conceptual and detailed design and may be the reason for the lack of tools with those unique features.

Implications of Methodological Problems

The methodological problems had an immediate effect on the beginning of the project. The design team had to modify the design strategy shortly after the work started. In addition, the team needed to look for a new design tool and then to actually improvise one. This caused a three-dimensional problem:

Schedule

The need for modified design strategy and tools imposed an urgent need to change the schedule of the first phase of the project. The times of the conceptual versus detailed design work and deliverable milestones had to be changed to match the realisation of the methodological strategy for a WAP-based interface. In addition, more time was required for the design team to look for and develop an appropriate design tool.

Communication

The methodological issues and their implications need to be communicated between the design team and the developer. However, the communications were "jammed" in two levels: First, the difference between conceptual and detailed design was not communicated properly. The design team that had changed its strategy towards the design framework assumed that the conceptual work was done. However, the client expected to get the concept with the full screen structure, including details of the screens. The understanding of the basic terms – Concept versus Detailed Design – was not communicated.

Second, the client expected to get the conceptual design according to the original schedule before approving the design to move on to the detailed design. However, the design team assumed that the schedule needed to be changed according to the different proportions between the conceptual and detailed design phases of the project. In addition, they expected approval of the concept before moving on. In fact, the schedule was not changed at that time and the original time slots and milestones slowly lost their meaning.

Perception

The seed for the differences in the perceptions of the schedule was planted at this very early phase of the project. The client perceived delays in the delivery of the concept, while the design team assumed that the concept was actually delivered ahead of schedule and that they should move on to the detailed design. The client was thus perceived as hesitant or unable to approve the concept and enable the progress of the project.

The Learning Curve Gets Longer

The initial problems discussed above started the "snowball" rolling. As time moved on and with additional time consuming problems, the schedule-snowball grew bigger and bigger. The learning of the system and the functional requirements took longer than originally expected. Both developer and design team had to learn the technology, the implications of the functional requirements, and the possible solutions, causing a longer learning curve. Beyond the methodological implications of the different technology, additional analyses on the part of the design team were required. The developers also learned more and more about what could and could not be done after the project started. The learning curves of the developer and the designers added more unplanned time to the original scheduling.

Changing Requirements

As with any dynamic development project, requirements changed along the way and added to the schedule problem. The developer learned and understood more with the progress of the work, and consequently original requirements continued changing. The implications of such changes were perceived differently by the developer and the designer. Because of slight differences between concept and detailed design, changes could have far reaching implications to the entire user interface structure. Thus, for the designer, many changes required conceptual changes which entailed many detailed design changes. However, the developer, who for a long time failed to understand the concept versus detailed design distinction, kept expecting each change to be solved and implemented within the design immediately. The different perceptions of the implications of changes complicated further the perceptions of how the project was progressing relative to the original schedule.

What Is an Important Change?

The developer treated a variety of required changes with equal importance and priority in a way that was not agreed upon with the designer. As mentioned above, some changes had far reaching implications and entailed conceptual and detailed design modifications. However, some changes were on the level of attached explanatory notes and terminology. The designer perceived these latter changes as less important, giving them a lower work priority. Since these changes were not delivered at the same pace as other changes, the gap between the developer's and the designer's perception of delivery times and delays further widened.

Project milestones, which sometimes impacted payment milestones, required deliverables approved by the client and the developer. In most cases, a deliverable constituted a major revision according to feedback or changing requirements by the developer. However, the different perception of the importance and priority of changes caused further differences in the definition of what constitutes a deliverable and approvable revision. In addition, the designers assumed that the delivery of a revision is considered a delivery for project tracking purposes. However, the developer insisted that an approved revision is one in which all changes and required corrections were implemented. While many delays were caused by this gap in how a revision was defined, it also introduced an emotional aspect of frustration and a deterioration of mutual trust.

Who Is the Real Stakeholder?

The liaison person appointed by the developer was not the only stakeholder in this project. Much of the communication between that person and the design team was not conveyed properly to the other stakeholders and decision makers within the development company. This additional link in the chain of communication and decision-making introduced both misunderstandings and further delays. The misunderstandings were on the level of agreements that were made and not approved by the management, corrections approved by the liaison but not by the stakeholders, and different priorities given by the management on the one hand and the liaison person on the other hand. In addition, the perception of delays received more magnitude with the stakeholders who were somewhat removed from the day-to-day process. They, in turn, applied more pressure on the liaison, which complicated the communication with the design team.

Personnel Changes

Personnel changes in the design team added complications on the personal level. The changes involved assigning a new team-mate to help the project leader. This new design team member turned out to be less appropriate for this specific project. However, this problem was recognised somewhat later, and some damage was already incurred. In addition, the design team tried to continue with the inappropriate person – hoping not to introduce further personnel changes. This was also a bad decision, since that team member did not contribute to the pressing schedule. Another problem which had a strong impact on the perceptions of the developer was that the design team leader had to leave the project for a week. This was perceived by the client as an additional cause for delays even though the actual work progressed during that week.

Communication Channels

One final factor that had an impact on the perceptions of the schedule was the communication channels between the developer and the design team. The primary channels were telephone conversations and e-mail discussions and deliveries. The least used channel was the personal meeting venue. The electronic channels are particularly prone to misunderstandings since they lack all the non-verbal factors that play an important role in inter-personal communications. The use of this particular communication channel, instead of having more frequent personal meetings, may have had some impact on the increasing gap in understanding between the developer and the design team, and possibly the inability to approve and decide in real time.

Summary: the Perception of Delays

The WAP-based user interface design project described in this chapter was viewed by the developer as having serious and damaging delays in its schedule. The delays can be accounted for by two main contributing factors summarized below:

1. In the first stages of the project, immediate methodological implications that were dealt with primarily by the user interface design team were misunderstood by the developer for a long time. Those initial gaps in the perceptions of factors affecting the schedule took their toll on the project's progression. The real impact was that the design team and the developer viewed and tracked the progress of the work on the timeline from different starting points.

2. As the project continued, different perceptions of schedule-affecting factors widened the gap created from the initial different starting points. Factors such as longer than expected learning times, many requirement changes, differing priorities to a variety of changes, lack of direct communication with the actual decision makers and inappropriate communication channels – all affected both real-time delays and perceived time delays.

At the bottom line, it seems that perceptions of the various factors that played a role in the progress of the project were different for the developer, on the one hand, and the design team on the other hand. Because of those different perceptions, the developer considered the project behind schedule and blamed the design team for damaging delays. On the other hand, such assertions were surprising to the design team since they perceived their work as being mostly on time.

Lessons Learned

Many lessons can be learned from this case in which a developing company commissioned user interface consultants to design the user interface. It is particularly applicable for projects with new technologies and platforms unfamiliar to either the developer and/or the user interface designers.

Initial Scheduling: Learn What You Need To Learn

When dealing with new and unfamiliar technologies and platforms (e.g. cellular phone, PDAs), allocate extra time – about the equivalent duration of the analysis phase – for learning the technological context. This period should not be a part of the schedule of the project itself. It should rather serve both parties to better evaluate the time needed for the work and, based on a mutual understanding of the time needed, determine a more accurate and reliable schedule for the project. Such a schedule should provide more time for the learning period once the project time line starts. It should also enable the exploration and development of design tools appropriate for the possible unique needs of the project.

Changes and Revision Policy: Work Out What "Important" Means

Functional requirements can be defined better, assuming that there is a better understanding of the implications of the new technology. This can and should enable the developer's commitment to the requirements delivered to the design team. Fewer changes to the requirements throughout the project will obviously cause less misunderstanding and fewer time delays.

Freezing requirements can be problematic for contemporary dynamic development projects. In such cases there should be a clear policy for changes and revisions. Both developer and designer need to understand and define a change and its importance and priority, on the one hand, and what is considered a deliverable revision, on the other hand. A good simple tool for that would be a list of all required changes along with their priorities and delivery schedule to be monitored by both designer and developer.

Identify Stakeholders

The definition of stakeholders should be expanded. The developers, on the one hand, and the design team, on the other hand, should be considered as part of the project's stakeholders. Thus, in addition to managers and investors and all the decision makers, all the developers and all of the consulting parties should be added to the stakeholder definition. The communications within this stakeholder definition can thus flow with fewer links in the chain and with shorter response times. In addition, any personnel changes can thus be considered as changes of stakeholders and be dealt with appropriately.

Maintain Communications

Virtual digital collaborative communication in development projects is very popular, however, it still lacks the personal touch. Most digital collaborative platforms are still asynchronous, and as such can cause misunderstandings and delays. By definition, it does not enable real-time decisions which are critical in time-constrained projects (and most are). In addition, the non-verbal aspects of human communication can be an important added-value to the clarity of the communication and the ability for decision making. (As an aside, in the final stages of the process, all communications took place face-to-face, enabling us to "close" issues faster and with fewer misunderstandings.)

Deal with Perceptions

Finally, be aware of the psychology and the human aspect of the project. Most elements and processes are basically made from our perceptions. Almost all aspects of the development process can be perceived differently by different people. In addition, organizational and social context affect perceptions. Thus, each side in the process should be aware that the other side may have a different perception and understanding of the same factor. Such awareness should prompt more communication to narrow the potential gaps in the perceptions.

PART 2

A New Usability for New Applications: Adapting Our Skills, Growing Our Role

"I Enjoyed That *This* Much!" Techniques for Measuring Usability in Leisure-Oriented Applications

5

Patrizia Marti and Paola Lanzi

Usability evaluation traditionally places a special emphasis on the need to develop software that is usable, i.e. used by "specified users to achieve specified goals with effectiveness, efficiency and satisfaction in a specified context of use" (ISO 9241, part 11). But what exactly does it mean to "achieve a goal" in the context of software applications for art, entertainment and leisure? Most activities in these contexts are not guided by a predefined objective based on user intention, instead, the leisure experience is a case in which individuals frequently "adjust" the way they interact with the environment, depending on many different and context-dependent factors. This chapter describes an approach to leisure-oriented usability evaluation developed around a handheld electronic museum tour guide, part of the Hyper Interaction within Physical Space (HIPS) project. It suggests that emotion, culture and context are important influences on perceived usability, and suggests how to apply these to usability away from the work environment.

Introduction

A visit to a museum is "a non-goal oriented" activity: since people can be pushed just by curiosity or pleasure, their behaviour is not predictable and their needs are "situated". When visiting a museum, individuals generally do not anticipate alternative courses of action, or their consequences, until some courses of action are already under way. In this chapter, we present a multidimensional approach based on scenarios and storytelling that includes four complementary levels: phenomenological, cognitive, emotive and sociocultural.

● At the phenomenological level the performance measure concerns the overt human behaviour and patterns of actions.

● At the cognitive level the performance measure concerns the cognitive effort associated with the use of technological tools that can support the experience of art.

● At the emotive level the performance measure concerns frustration, confusion, satisfaction, engagement.

● At the socio-cultural level the performance measure concerns the cultural impact of the content and the way it is presented (narrative styles, voices and accents); and the level of support in the case of cooperative activities in a group (communication, knowledge sharing, collective memories).

A central concept of our approach to leisure-oriented system evaluation is the importance of not only the actions of "users", but also the contexts in which these actions take place, including the sociocultural context of the interaction, the physical environment and the personal experience. It is this context that shapes the relationship between human actions and system outcomes. However, this link is not a simple one. Some features of the system may induce errors or confusion, or troublesome configurations of the external environment may occur that the system does not minimise. For example, *affordances* of cultural settings play a central role in shaping the interaction. These include:

● properties that are intrinsically connected to a particular setting such as the width of an exhibit, its position, its artistic importance;

● architectural elements like access points to a room, arches and steps;

● dynamic and contextual configurations of elements present in the space (crowd, lights).

The role of *affordances* in attracting the visitor can be hampered when combined with certain configurations (e.g. crowding or poor lighting often oblige the visitor to skip important exhibits). A good leisure-oriented system should try to minimise the effects of configurations which prevent visitors from viewing some exhibits in the museum, making it necessary to analyse the richness of the context of interaction when discussing usability and engagement.

The importance of "context of use" for design and evaluation of interactive systems has been the subject of considerable research in both the HCI and the computer-supported co-operative work (CSCW) literature (Nardi, 1996; Hutchins, 1995). Carroll (1995) was amongst the first to question the appropriateness of the task (defined as "what a user should do to reach a certain goal"), as the main unit of analysis for system design and evaluation. Instead, he introduced the concept of scenarios as representations of activity that are intended to capture rich aspects of the context of interaction. However, situations exist where it is not possible to define detailed scenarios since the activity that the system must support is mostly unpredictable.

This is the case of the visit to a museum or to art settings in general, where the behaviour of the visitors depends on variables that are difficult to anticipate and control. Indeed to have a realistic idea of the use of the system, the visitor should be free to explore the environment and assess the level of support of the system in pursuing objectives that can arise during the visit. The behaviour of the system cannot be evaluated on the basis of fully predefined scenarios of use: what it is possible to do, however, is to generate circumstances that can affect the human-system interaction, such as crowd or time pressure (closing time of the museum) and observe how the visitor uses the system to face these circumstances. At this point, the interpretation of the observed behaviour becomes crucial. This is the reason why we propose a narrative approach based on scenarios and storytelling which involves users in the process of system evaluation through a participatory interpretation of the findings.

Multidimensional Evaluation Based on Story Telling and Scenarios

The interest in narratives has a long tradition. Bruner (1990) considers narrative a primitive function of human psychology, lying at the heart of human thought. The representation of experience in narratives provides a frame which enables humans to interpret their experiences. In this way narrative is a fundamental aspect in the construction of meaning.

Although narratives have been studied in many areas of psychology, the idea of exploiting them for system design and evaluation is quite recent and still not consolidated (Erickson, 1995). It is based on the need to understand user requirements through the collection of implicit knowledge that a user may have gained through experience. In particular, the use of narratives for system evaluation does not aim to provide quantitative results but to structure a framework within with users may express knowledge otherwise difficult to verbalize. Stories make it possible to study the complexity of the context (media, internal/external environment, actors); details about critical events that can be observed very seldom; personal involvement; emotional details; and the concreteness and veracity of personal experiences.

This chapter applies the narrative approach to the evaluation of an electronic tourist guide. The evaluation was carried out in an Italian museum, the Museo Civico, in Siena, with real visitors recruited at the museum entrance. The tourist guide is a prototype system developed within a project called Hyper Interaction within Physical Space (HIPS),[1] funded by the European Commission within the I-Cube (I³) Programme. The system is very advanced since it exploits cutting edge technologies (positioning technology, dynamic language generation) and visionary interaction design concepts (access to the information space through the physical movement in the museum; user modelling for content adaptation).

The system guides visitors by generating audio messages: users can get instructions on how to find items of interest, hear descriptions with references to items seen earlier and to ones that will follow, or ask for additional information. Information is generated dynamically, adaptive, and integrated with maps and spatial directions. When interacting with users, the system integrates their requests with a customized user-model, the user's browsing history, and their physical location at the moment of the query, providing highly contextual and personalized information (Marti et al., in press). The information content varies according to the user's location, preferences, and to the information already given. From a hardware point of view the system is based on a client-server model; the clients that visitors carry around are pen-driven palmtop computers with a screen, headphones and no keyboard. Localization is performed by various means: infrared, radio and GPS (Global Positioning System). Connectivity to the server is wireless.

Multiple Levels of Interaction, Multiple Levels of Performance Measure

The evaluation of such a system was quite complex because of installation problems within the museum's infrastructure, specific features of the

---

[1] HIPS Consortium: University of Siena (I) – Project Coordinator, University of Edinburgh (UK), University College of Dublin (IR); IRST (I), GMD (D), SINTEF (N); ALCATEL (I).

system, and its particular context of use. For these reasons and in order to address the multi-faceted components of the HIPS system, we decided to adopt a multidimensional approach based on storytelling and scenarios. Specifically, we assessed user performance on four levels: phenomenological, cognitive, emotive and sociocultural.

At the phenomenological level the performance measure concerns included:

- Users' perception of the adaptation to the visiting style (personalization of the information, pauses, pace of narration) and the physical movement as a primary means for accessing information.
- Auditory comments (deictics, pronouns, etc) effectiveness in supporting the users' orientation and recognition of artworks.
- Tool flexibility (skill of personalizing and contextualizing the information according to the users' changes of path or visiting style).

At the cognitive level the performance measure concerns focused on:

- The cognitive effort associated with the use of the tool and the comprehension of the contents.
- Users' conceptual model.

At this level, scenarios were used to question the design of the system. We used Norman's cycle of cognition based on: goals, intentions, planning, execution, perception and evaluation to generate questions such as "How does the artefact evoke goals in the user?" or "How does the artefact make it easy or difficult to carry out the activity?" or "How does the artefact support the user when a shift in the goal occurs?".

At the emotive level the performance measure mainly concerned aspects of experiential cognition:

- Observation of frustration.
- Observation of confusion.
- Expression of satisfaction.
- Expression of engagement.

At the socio-cultural level the performance measure concerns included:

- The social aspects of group activity mediated by the system (communication, knowledge sharing, collective memories).

- Appraisal /dislike of contents.

- Impact of narrative styles (male/female voices, accents, music, reading styles).

Even if the narrative approach impacted the evaluation at the four above mentioned levels, it is worth clarifying that the stories mostly provided the structuring framework for reasoning on the system and externalizing implicit knowledge. For the evaluation of more detailed features of the system, from interaction design to contents, we complemented storytelling with other methodologies, including ethnographic observations of the activity and laboratory testing (heuristic evaluation, cognitive walkthrough, scenario-based evaluation on intermediate prototypes (Nielsen and Mack, 1994)).

Preparation of Test Material, Equipment and Test Procedure

We needed four staff people to perform the test:

- a technician who took care of the correct system functioning and the data log;

- an observer who took notes using an observation grid and recorded user comments on an audio tape;

- an interviewer who recruited the visitors, introduced the system, supported during the test and facilitated during the storytelling;

- a video operator who video recorded the test.

Next, we organized the test procedure into these steps:

- recruiting visitors at the entrance of the museum, who volunteered to try the system;

- briefing users on the system and its basic functionality;

- conducting pre-test interview to collect data about the users' character-istics;

- describing the test procedure;

- carrying out a test session in the form of a free exploration and re-creating, when possible, pre-defined scenarios (to induce the users to try a specific functionality the interface, to try the system under particular circumstances or constraints);

- storytelling.

User Sampling

The subjects who took part in the evaluation were recruited in the museum on the day of the test. They were chosen at random from a group of museum visitors who had already volunteered to try the system and participate in a debriefing after the test. All subjects were English or English-speaking tourists and were picked to span different characteristics:

- Age: 15–18; 19–25, 25–30, 31–40, 41–50, 51–60, 61 and over.

- Nationality.

- Average/very good knowledge of English.

- Gender: males and females.

- Poor/average/very good knowledge of art.

- Previous knowledge of Museo Civico: yes/no; in case, how many times the user visited the museum, and how long ago.

Test Session

The evaluation at the four levels was carried out on the basis of direct observation of user activity (video recorded) during the free exploration and scenarios execution. We used scenarios to create a context for the activity, and we artificially provoked users to evaluate the system under specific conditions or exceptional constraints. Such conditions included:

- Time slots for the visit (near the closing time).

- Museum crowd.

- Distribution of physical *affordances* in the environment (chairs, light conditions, location of signs, presence of maps).

- Single /group visit.

- Use of other artefacts (book guide, audio guide, paper maps, etc.).

The test provided us with a variety of observed data including:

- Time spent in front of each exhibit.

- Time spent in the museum.

- Observation of frustration, confusion, satisfaction, engagement.

- Conformity with a pre-defined visiting style (paths defined on the basis of explicit interactions with the PDA).

- Possible changes in the visiting style.

- Influence of physical *affordances* (e.g. objects, light, people in front of a specific exhibit).

Further data came from the system log of the interaction with the PDA interface: list of descriptions heard; typology of descriptions heard; number and type of commands used.

Post-Test Session: Storytelling

At the end of each session, the visitors were involved in a debriefing (in one of the rooms of the museum) where storytelling was encouraged to further comment, analyse, and interpret events which occurred during the test. The subjects were asked to describe their experience looking at the video recording of the test. This created a common base of discussion and knowledge, and provided concrete data to express impressions and points of view. To facilitate the storytelling, we prepared a set of questions to stimulate the discussion at the four levels of evaluation. These questions spanned over the following dimensions:

- Global experience

- Satisfaction /engagement.

- Contents.

- Design concepts.

As a general outcome of the evaluation, we can say that stories mostly addressed aspects related to the emotional and socio-cultural levels. Indeed the system created a rich sensory environment that the users perceived but were not able to describe in a more structured form than stories. Stories, being concrete and immediate, do not require abstraction or introspection, so the users were free to tell and to compare their previous experiences, re-creating a context to share with the facilitators. That is why we used story-telling as an expressive means to stimulate communication between people who were not familiar with each other and to encourage them to speak about personal feelings, experiences and impressions.

We were aware that this kind of evaluation cannot provide quantitative data about satisfaction and engagement (such as that obtained using the Differential Emotions Scale, the Semantic Differential Scale or the free labelling method (Kim and Moon, 1998)). However, since the system was oriented to entertainment and leisure, we decided to collect data that could give insights into the capability of the system to intrigue and attract the users. During the debriefing we collected a corpus of about 20 stories that were mapped on user requirements and system specifications. Here is one of those stories:

> When we went to Avignone, to visit the Palais des Papes, we had a local guide, a teacher of a school party who explained in detail the artistic and historical features of every room. We were interested in her explanation, but the students (children of the primary school) got suddenly tired. During the visit we passed through a room, where there was a different kind of exhibition where strange and funny animals dangled from the ceiling. Pupils were very curious to know about them, but the teacher was prepared only on the Palais des Papes, so she passed through the room without paying any attention to the animals of the exhibition.

The story contains a number of relevant elements for the design and evaluation. It highlights that visitors have heterogeneous needs: most of the time their activity is "non-goal oriented" since they can be pushed just by curiosity or pleasure, and their behaviour is not predictable. They often do not know ahead of time, or with any specificity, what future state they desire to bring about. Therefore, the situations of use can be various and idiosyncratic, leading the visitors to frequently adjust their goals and objectives during the visit.

Taking these elements into account, we can infer that the HIPS tour guide and systems like it must learn to adapt to visitor inclinations as they arise. The solution designed into the system, which proved to be particularly appropriate in this respect, focused on establishing a closer link between environment and user interactivity through the introduction of adaptive mechanisms.

Lessons Learned

Most people measure usability by watching users perform various tasks efficiently and correctly. New systems such as entertainment or edutainment systems, are not necessarily designed to help users perform work tasks or to save time (Höök, et al., 1999). In some cases it is exactly the opposite: the system should encourage the users to stay longer and enjoy the interaction. Usability evaluation in these contexts is oriented to more "soft" characteristics, like the engagement, the emotional involvement, and cultural habits. Therefore, new approaches have to be envisaged to assess the impact of such systems on users.

The narrative approach to evaluation is a promising contribution toward this new challenge, revealing through narratives some of the "softer" features related to the experiential dimension of contact with art. We learned some key points from this experience.

Context of evaluation is vital. Working "in the field" makes it possible to collect a body of reliable data in the natural context of use, avoiding the artificial environment of the laboratory. However, an evaluation in context imposes a set of constraints that made the tests difficult to execute and, in some cases, the results difficult to interpret. These include the restriction of the opening and closing time of the museum, incoming disturbing factors like the curiosity of other visitors and crowd, that impacted on the evaluation.

There are no easily defined user models which describe visitors to a museum (or people engaging in any other form of leisure activity). Notwithstanding the pre-test interview where we tried to know more about the users (background, interests, knowledge of the museum, age, etc.), with the short time at disposal and without storytelling we could not really understand the impact that specific design concepts could have on the particular visitor.

The role of the facilitator during the debriefing sessions with the visitors was crucial. The facilitator had to guide the discussion focusing the attention of the subjects on critical aspects like the role of the others as resources of information, the role of other artefacts like a book guide as mediator of the activity, the specific configuration of the space and the context of the visit. Our structuring theoretical framework of reference for this was "distributed cognition" (Hutchins, 1995) that allowed us to understand, with respect to a wide unit of analysis, how cognition is distributed and evolved in such a complex environment.

The narrative approach was oriented to providing qualitative data that were open to interpretation. However, most of the interpretation was done with the users and enabled us to stimulate discussion and the sharing of different view points; whilst also minimising the pressure to present data in terms of numbers and percentages.

In summary, the study described in this chapter is a contribution toward the compelling yet difficult nature of evaluation of entertainment or edutainment systems. The idea of focusing on "soft" characteristics and use storytelling to evaluate their impact on the user is in turn a methodological step ahead and a source of inspiration for design.

References

Bruner JS (1990) Acts of meaning. Harvard University Press Cambridge, MA.

Carroll JM (ed.) (1995). Scenario-based design: envisioning work and technology in system development. Wiley, New York.

Erickson T (1995) Notes on Design Practice: Stories and Prototypes as Catalysts for Communication. In: John M Carroll Scenario-Based Design: Envisioning Work and Technology in System Development, pp 37–58

Höök K, Persson P, Holm J, Tullgren K, Sjölinder M, Karlgren J (1999) Spatial or Narrative: A study of the Agneta & Frida system , Workshop on Affect in Interactions: Towards a New Generation of Interfaces, held during i3 Conference in Siena, October, 1999

Hutchins E (1995) Cognition in the Wild. MIT Press, London.

Kim J, Moon JY (1998) Designing Emotional Usability in Customer Interfaces – Trustworthiness of Cyber-Banking System Interfaces. Interacting with Computers, 10:1–29

Marti P, Gabrielli L, Pucci F. 'Situated Interaction in Art,' Personal and Ubiquitous Computing (2001), 5: 71–74, Springer-Verlag, London.

Nardi BA (1996) Context and consciousness: Activity theory and human-computer interaction. Cam: MIT Press

Nielsen J, Mack RL (1994) (eds) Usability Inspection Methods. John Wiley, New York

Caught Between Real and Virtual Worlds

Phil Turner and Susan Turner

This chapter describes how we, as HCI practitioners, contributed to the design of a collaborative virtual environment-based simulator. This simulator is to be used by senior maritime professionals to practice and acquire safety-critical skills through simulated training. In the course of this work we encountered a number of unanticipated design and evaluation challenges beyond "simple" usability, though, of course, evaluating the usability of virtual environments is far from simple. The first of these challenges, or tensions, involved the need to exploit the power and possibilities of a collaborative virtual environment to the full against the need to maintain the fidelity of the modelled environment. The second challenge is more subtle, given that a virtual environment can only be an approximation to reality, how approximate should it be, or "how real is real?".

The Challenge: Can Virtual Systems Solve Real Problems?

The focus of the HCI intervention described in this chapter was the DISCOVER project. This project comprised a tight, well focused consortium of end-users and software developers and had as its aim the development, deployment and evaluation of a collaborative virtual environment (CVE)-based training environment. The rationale for the project was essentially two-fold: first, there is a well established need to train senior professionals in the maritime and offshore sectors in the management of safety-critical situations. Here we are referring to high-level command and control skills rather than, say, fire fighting. Second, training at present is very costly and reducing costs is, unsurprisingly, popular with all concerned. Current training requires the senior professionals to attend courses delivered at a specialist training site for up to a week with all of the cost associated with being away from work. Despite this inconvenience it is clear that those involved take the training very seriously and it is not unusual for them to give up holidays to attend specific courses.

At the end of 1999, the project, which is supported by the European Commission, was reallocated from a "technology" section of the Commission to one which had a different focus and philosophy, namely a strong emphasis on user involvement and "user friendliness". This new section insisted that the intended end-users of the DISCOVER be placed at the centre of the development process. As a result the project was presented with a short deadline in which to take the necessarily remedial action. The Commission suggested that they recruit a partner with expertise in this domain to help. We (the authors) were invited as HCI practitioners to "fix the problem".

The DISCOVER Vision

The DISCOVER "vision" was to provide trainers and trainees with the opportunity to train and practice their safety-critical and command and control skills at their place of work whether it be at sea or on an oil platform. DISCOVER will deliver this training by way of a collaborative virtual environment running over the Internet. The overall DISCOVER system comprises a web-based training administration system where a trainee can register, review their progress and launch either theory based modules or the CVE itself. The project envisages a trainee logging into the administration system, and then brushing up on their command and control skills in the theory module area before practising those skills on line by entering the CVE. The CVE may be running on the ship's own network, or be hosted on shore or also be running in a truly distributed fashion across the trainee's organization or the wider world. Needless to say this is quite ambitious.

Our Brief: "Develop a Highly Usable VR System – and Do It Yesterday!"

The project had identified a number of key areas which needed specialist attention. These were to:

- Produce a definitive statement of requirements on the DISCOVER system from the training organization. This involved understanding the methods used in current training, which ranged from state-of-the-art physical simulators costing tens of millions of pounds, to simple role playing, and their methods of assessment.

- Adopt a suitable pedagogic model for the training environment.

- Understand how we were to validate the DISCOVER system with the appropriate validating bodies. The project had ambitions to sell the system across the world to a number of shipping and oil companies and thus required a suitable seal of approval.

- Produce for the software designers a detailed description of the virtual environments to be modelled and a list of the objects and their behaviours therein.

- Specify a collaborative virtual environment with a strong emphasis on fidelity and usability.

- Match the system to current and proposed training scenarios.

And we had three months to complete this in the first instance!

Phase 1: Just What Should a Virtual Training System Do?

Some requirements work had been carried out before our entry to the project, but this had simply taken the form of the collection of high level statements of intent from the training companies and lists of competencies (or skills) to be trained. This provided our first political advantage: working closely with managers and training personnel in the user companies *in itself* convinced these project partners that their needs were being seriously considered. Thus our activities tended to be viewed in a constructive and receptive way. We will not provide a detailed description of the techniques we used, since they are familiar ones, but we employed a combination of interviews with trainees, trainers, their managers, observation and video-recording of training sessions and the collection of relevant documenta-tion. All this took place at user sites. Again, goodwill was generated simply by the amount of effort very clearly being devoted to the user-centred work.

The results of this fieldwork fed into a large group of requirements relating to the way in which CVE based training could best be used in its particular intended context. Fortunately, although CVE design is a young field, there is an emerging body of literature which addresses generic usability issues for single users (e.g. Stanney et al., 1998; Sutcliffe et al., 2000) and in the collaborative context, the guidelines provided by the COVEN project (Normand et al., 1999). Thus we were able to supplement our own primary findings with secondary material from the literature and produce a large body of user-related requirements material in a relatively short time.

The Use of the MoSCoW Method

At this stage we had a large set of requirements in clear need of prioritization. In keeping with the user-centred philosophy which we had started to foster, this would be done in conjunction with the user companies. The MoSCoW technique from the Dynamic Systems Development Method – DSDM, (Stapleton, 1997) afforded a means of doing this which would be readily understandable to users and familiar to the developer partners in the project. DSDM prioritizes requirements using the MoSCoW rules.

The uppercase letters of the acronym (the o's are only there to make for a memorable acronym) stand for: Must have for requirements that are fundamental to the system. Without them the system will be unworkable and useless. The Must have category defines the minimum usable subset. Should have for important requirements for which there is a work-around in the short term but the system will be useful and usable without them. Could have for requirements that can more easily be left out of the current development. Want to have but won't have this time round for those valuable requirements that can wait till later development takes place. A small sample of the prioritised requirements follows below. A substantial subset of the higher priority lists related to usability and other non-functional concerns.

Must	Should	Could	Want
The ability for trainers to increase stress in a safe, controlled manner for the trainees.	Provide a more satisfying professional role for trainers than classroom teaching.	Courses *formally* validated by the appropriate standards bodies.	Measures of training transfer.

By now, therefore, we had an substantial body of organized and prioritized requirements which formed the main body of the requirements and evaluation deliverables to the funding body. These reports passed their review, user-related concerns were accepted as the main force driving the design of the software and the project moved forward.

Phase 2: Hello, I'm Your Avatar

A prototype system was created and demonstrated to trainers and prospective trainees at all three maritime training sites. In use each trainee begins by adopting a role – captain, chief engineer, first mate and so forth. They then put on a lightweight set of combined headphones and microphone to afford communication with other avatars and the trainer. Once a minimum of two trainees have entered the system, the trainer, who has been overseeing this process, starts the training scenario (*Fig. 6.1*). Avatars are able to communicate with one another by way of (virtual) radio and (virtual) telephone and are able to walk and run, open doors and pick up and operate fire extinguishers.

The trainer (or trainers) have all these facilities but have the God-like powers of being able to watch all trainees simultaneously, set fires and so forth as can be seen in *Fig. 3.2*. The training itself consists of working through a detailed scenario, usually drawn from a real world incident, which requires the trainees to role play and collectively deal with the problems which arise during the course of playing it out. At the end of the training, the trainer will debrief those involved and may use the play-back facilities of the DISCOVER CVE to illustrate particular points.

Figure 6.1 Two trainees (avatars) on the virtual bridge

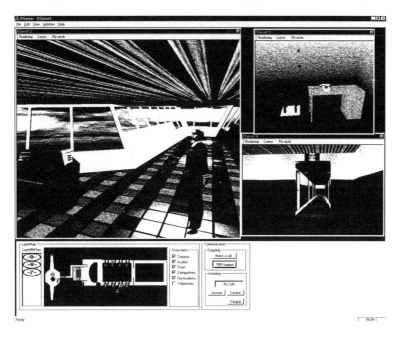

Figure 6.2 The tutor's user interface

Demonstrations of the software and simple hands-on tasks were followed by interviews and questionnaires. Our intention was to give potential end users a clearer impression of what a CVE is, how it could be used, to elicit feedback which could be used to refine requirements. We had also evidently managed to convince our developers of the importance of usability issues, since they were particularly keen to have any problems of this sort identified. However, our intentions were confounded by the very prominence which usability assumed in these initial trials. Eager for early feedback, and understandably reluctant to undertake development which might be misdirected, our technologists delivered a prototype just as soon as the software could be run independently of its development environment. This meant that although a reasonable impression could be gained of the functionality which could be offered, user interaction was in a very immature state. As a consequence, finer grain usability issues, for example the ability to identify the focus of an avatar's gaze, were obscured by larger difficulties such as moving through the environment. Equally users could not be induced to speculate in depth about how the system might be used, or how training delivered through such a medium might relate to existing practice. For example, it is difficult to convince the captain of one of the world's largest passenger vessels of the possibilities of the new medium after difficulty with movement control has "trapped" him for some minutes in a corner of the virtual bridge. However, some indications did emerge of the type of usage envisaged in each training context, and much debate was triggered about the detailed design features which would be necessary to support these.

The developers now urgently required a unified, detailed, concrete design specification which would nonetheless support each intended context of use. This was to be achieved by means of a workshop involving each of the three maritime organizations. (There was only one offshore organization in the project, whose requirements were relatively unified and straightforward.)

Phase 3: Virtual Reality Meets Paper and Pen

At this two-day event, trainers from the three organizations met with the representatives from one of the software developer organizations and two facilitators from the requirements team.

The agenda was very simple: to agree the detailed functionality of the maritime simulator and how it was expected to be used. We adapted elements of Contextual Design (Holtzblatt and Beyer, 1998) to facilitate these processes, principally a variant of the affinity diagram technique, which supports the identification of common themes from a mass of contextual data. We began by asking each training organization to revisit what they wanted of DISCOVER in terms of the "w" words (familiar to user-centred design practitioners), i.e. why, when, who, where and of course, how. As each organization described their needs we recorded each issue or explicit requirement on a Post-IT® note. At the end of the process we had gathered over 400 Post-ITs of which approximately 10 per cent were subsequently discarded as duplicates or irrelevant on closer inspection.

The trainers were then invited to create an affinity model which required them to sort the requirements/issues into logical groups (as illustrated in *Fig. 6.3*): emerging groupings included the layout and configuration of the virtual ship, the appearance and functionality of the avatars and the context of use of the completed system. Throughout this process the software designer helped ground the requirements in reality. Informal discussion with the three trainers afterwards revealed that they thought that the day had gone well. The use of the Post-Its and their grouping was a familiar technique from other contexts, and had fostered engagement and apparent consensus. At the end of the first day we had succeeded in co-constructing an affinity model and subsequently a communications model and an artefact/physical model (ibid.) of the environment to be created.

Figure 6.3 *Maritime trainers creating an affinity diagram*

Caught Between Real and Virtual Worlds

While agreement was breaking out at this workshop, so too were some concerns. As most HCI practitioners would agree, the distinction between design and evaluation in HCI is often blurred, indeed design and evaluation have been described as the different sides of the same coin. The design of the DISCOVER system proved to be no different. As we elicited requirements and undertook early design we kept an eye on evaluation, ultimately as a sanity check. The use of the prototype, described above, had given us clear usability requirements. The affinity diagram had given us detailed requirements of the design, content and substance of the DISCOVER collaborative virtual environment but concerns as to the issue of evaluation (and with it validation) began to emerge.

Design Tensions: No Magic, Thanks

For many collaborative tasks in virtual environments, the goal is to achieve a particular state of affairs within the virtual world, for example agreeing the layout of an office, as in Hindmarsh et al. (1998). For others, the activity within the CVE is part of a larger collaborative process, but the way collaboration works within the CVE need not exactly replicate real world interaction. In contrast, the DISCOVER environment must support the acquisition of real world skills. In short, skills acquired in the DISCOVER CVE must be transferable to the real world of the ship. This presents a significant constraint: ideally, interaction and collaboration must not be artificially *harder* or *take longer* than in the real world, but neither must they be artificially *easier* or executed *faster*. Thus the design of DISCOVER should treat with caution "magical" devices such as birds' eye views of the state of environment, *Star Trek*-like transporting, or visible rubber banding between an avatar and its current focus of attention.

Accordingly, much research which has addressed the problems of ensuring that the users of such environments are aware of their surroundings and of other users cannot be employed directly. Consider, for example, the problems with recognizing other avatars. To maintain realism, avatars cannot be simply labelled. There may also be the presence of dense smoke, and perhaps the need for the avatars to wear vision obscuring breathing apparatus. All of this means that recognizing one's colleagues (as avatars), mediated in the real situation by such characteristics as gait, stance and minor variations in standard issue clothing, becomes far more difficult.

Thus there is a fundamental tension between exploiting the technology to the full to produce a state-of-the-art virtual training environment and creating one which is faithful to the behaviour and constraints of a real ship. This, of course, is not merely a design issue but also presents a corresponding evaluation challenge.

Design Tensions: Virtually Real or Really Real?

In addition to the technical challenges of designing and implementing this collaborative system, there are the more subtle issues of convincing senior professionals and their employers that the system is easy to use, is appropriately realistic and will deliver the training they require. Would you trust the captain of your passenger ferry who has practised his command and control skills on something which looks suspiciously like an arcade game? Similarly, would you, as personnel manager of a large shipping company buy this product and expect to have your ships' captains to use it?

The DISCOVER trainers believed that the collaborative virtual environment should aim to model a ship as fully and as accurately as possible to bridge this credibility gap. However, we recognize that the DISCOVER presentation of reality must necessarily fail, as it is likely that even small limitations will shatter the illusion. So the design challenge is to identify and abstract from reality those elements which will give a sufficiently good impression of a ship. But how real is real? To date, existing research has focused on achieving a sense of presence and evaluation instruments have been developed to measure just that, but what has not been established is whether "presence" is a good measure of being real. During our requirements work at one of the partners' sites in Denmark, a trainer told us that when a mariner was using their physical simulator they spoke of it as being "their ship" within 30 minutes of use. Physical simulators in contrast to a collaborative virtual environment are equipped with real, physical controls, readouts, charts and manuals with a synthetic display: for CVEs, all is synthetic.

Evaluating Reality?

From a functional perspective, the environment must (for example) be robust, adequately fast, allow the movement of trainees and their interaction with each other and various objects, support trainer–trainee interaction, the modification of the environment by trainees and provide the numerous other functions specified in the requirements. Evaluation of such features is *relatively* simple, through inspection against the requirements list combined with simple trials covering the actions necessary to support the training scenarios. Narrow usability evaluation is again fairly unproblematic. Initially, we have used expert cognitive walkthroughs based on the structure suggested by the COVEN project, extended to cover aspects of usability for pedagogic interaction. These results are supplemented by the administration to representative users undertaking task-based trials of Kalawsky's VRUSE questionnaire instrument (Kalawsky, 1999), with additional material to elicit data about usability for collaboration. We are left with the questions, "However how does one evaluate reality?" and "Is presence an appropriate measure?". At the time of writing we are left with a round of iterative evaluation and redesign to determine whether the system is sufficiently real.

Lessons Learned and Tentative Recommendations

- Despite the user centred design approach we adopted, it turned out that the real issue was one of selective translation from the old to the new simulated environment. However the question we are still struggling to answer is "Which bits to translate?".

- The related lesson is that of distinguishing different aims relating to reality or fidelity in virtual environments. DISCOVER had at least two such aims: to convince prospective purchasers (and others) of the apparent usefulness of the system and to be effective as a training environment. The requirements relating to these aims not identical.

- Use the MoSCoW method to prioritize requirements. This is invaluable and is popular with software developers and users.

- Two points on the use of prototypes: take great care when working with early prototypes as poor usability can so easily obscure their potential to generate requirements. While the usefulness of prototypes is well known we would particularly stress their importance when the gap between the current and new system is large.

References

Hindmarsh J, Frazer M, Heath C, Benford S and Greenhalgh C (1998) Fragmented Interaction: establishing mutual orientation in virtual environments. In: Proceedings of CSCW'98 ACM Press, New York

Holtzblatt K and Beyer H (1998) Contextual Design: defining customer-centred systems Morgan Kaufman, New York

Normand V, Babski C, Benford S, Bullock A, Carion S, Chrysanthou Y et al. (1999) The COVEN project: exploring applicative, technical and usage dimensions of collaborative virtual environments, PRESENCE: Teleoperators and Virtual Environment 8(2):218–236

Stanney KM, Mourant MM and Kennedy JS (1998) Human Factors Issues in Virtual Environments: A Review of the Literature. PRESENCE: Teleoperators and Virtual Environments 7(4):327–351

Stapleton J (1997) DSDM: Dynamic Systems Development Method Addison-Wesley, London.

Sutcliffe AG and Kaur KD (2000) Evaluating the usability of virtual reality interfaces, Behaviour and Information Technology 19(6):415–426

The XMod Files: Defining and Designing the "User Experience" 7

George M Donahue

IntElegant, a leading Internet consultancy employing nearly 3,000 people, assembled what may be the largest group ever to focus on the user experience when it put together XMod. IntElegant's Experience Modelling (XMod) group represents a new, holistic, "seamless" approach to user-experience research, one that seeks to apply insights gained about users to business and market strategy as well as to user-interface design. XMod employs techniques derived from the social sciences, marketing and human computer interaction. This chapter outlines the emergence of XMod and its unique approach to usability and related disciplines, and discusses both the difficulties and benefits of attempting to define and design "user experience". All company names have been changed throughout.

Introduction: User Experience Modelling Becomes a Discipline

As of January 2001, 105 people, working out of ten different offices in four different continents made up IntElegant's Experience Modelling (XMod) discipline. IntElegant created XMod in late 1999 by acquiring En Vivo and merging its existing user research group with the acquisition. XMod may be the largest group of people ever brought together by a single company to focus on user experience.

"IntElegant is not the only company concerned with user experience, nor the only one to employ an ethnographic stance, nor the only one to centrally value user-centred design. However, we are clearly the only company to develop this capability on this scale and to deploy it across all industries and geographies," notes IntElegant's chief experience officer (CXO).

As such departments often do at Internet consulting companies, XMod houses the company's usability and human-centred design (HCD) functions, for HCD is part of what XMod is about. But XMod's mandate also addresses other aspects of user experience. A draft version of the XMod Industry Handbook puts it like this: "At IntElegant, we believe that people want products and services that integrate neatly into their lives. For this reason, we provide our clients with user-centred strategies and solutions." The document explains that XMod's work paves the way for designing products and services that will be "familiar, intuitive, compelling, usable and useful for users, whether online or off."

This is a somewhat broader portfolio than many "traditional" user-experience groups have. The focus in most such groups is HCH, for example. XMod's mandate extends to strategy as well as design; a more appropriate term might be "human-centred business strategy." Whatever it is called, XMod intends to provide insight about users and customers (or whoever the specific interactants may be) that clients can use to discover new markets and opportunities. XMod is also about human-centred design, guiding product and user-interface design for client web and other offerings, so that those offerings will be useful, usable and compelling for users, and yield maximum value for the client.

The Emergence of XMod

IntElegant's CXO co-founded En Vivo, which IntElegant acquired in 1999. He described En Vivo as a "research and development consultancy for understanding experience, and turning that into a basis for product, service, and communication development." En Vivo worked closely with new-product design groups at client companies, many from the package goods, appliance, and automotive industries. En Vivo communicated its research findings via "experience models" – consumer profiles, scenarios, and video ethnographies, highlight tapes of consumers engaged in activities of interest, like driving an SUV, housecleaning, shaving or having a cold. Clients used the models as a basis for new product or campaign ideas they could then develop.

Upon acquisition, 40 or so former En Vivo staff joined a dozen IntElegant legacy user researchers, and so was created XMod. It merged two groups with different perspectives, vocabularies and techniques; they came from different discourse communities and theoretical traditions. "Research" was what both groups did, but their respective researches were tuned to different ends – real-world business strategy on one hand, and virtual-world design (of commercial web-sites, mainly) on the other.

At this point the multiple user-related disciplines of En Vivo and IntElegant merged under a single name – the birth of XMod. "We deliberately changed the name because we wanted to force ourselves and the company to rethink the role of the discipline," says the CXO. "We didn't just want to do ethno-graphic research. . . . Nor were we just going to do usability testing. We were hoping the two things would come together and be a seamless approach to research. We picked "modelling" as the discipline's name because it can mean models of experience, as well as models for experience. . . . XMod's objective is developing models of experience that are descriptive, prescrip-tive, or both."

XMod's purpose is to provide "profoundly useful information on the organi-zation of experience and how products, communications, business models, and new technology affect it" to client companies and internal IntElegant teams. Key to this is XMod's "consistent theoretical approach toward the centrality of experience and the value of structural explanations, which allow it to employ, with consistency and flexibility, a wide range of methods for understanding how people interact with our clients and their products and services."

For a "structural explanation" of XMod, you need to see the discipline in terms of structuralism, a body of theory with roots in the work of nineteenth century Swiss linguist Fernand de Saussure. Saussure's influence went beyond linguistics; anthropology and literary criticism were especially receptive. Structuralism holds that to understand something – a culture, behaviours occurring within a culture, its art, language, etc. – you must study the behaviour or object within the appropriate socio-cultural context. For example, you study consumer behaviour in the context of capitalism, the economic "structure" it occurs within. Structuralists look for patterns and structures – in cultures, behaviours, practices, literatures and languages.

Techniques for User Experience Modelling

User experience modelling activities within XMod fall into five categories:

- *Thought leadership.* Activities may involve developing point-of-view statements for industries, or user-centred strategy and design expertise to clients and internal teams.

- *Research, analysis, and model-building.* XModelers may conduct field research in stores, homes, offices, on the street, etc., gathering experience data by observing and interviewing people in relevant contexts of use. Secondary research focuses on reviewing relevant literature on industries, products, services and trends. Model-building refers to activities that communicate insights into user experience that clients can use, for example, to better target marketing messages, identify gaps in product offerings, and in general, to provide clients with a robust and valu:able understanding of user behaviour, attitudes, beliefs, expectations, routines, needs and wants.

- *Idea generation and opportunity mapping.* These may take the form of sessions based on research and analysis that identify and prioritise opportunities. Audience-definition, segmentation, profiling and scenario activities also belong to this category.

- *Participatory design.* This and the following category include most of the human-centred design activities many readers will recognise, such as concept-testing, card-sorting, user- and task-analysis, and prototyping; the information architecture, task-flow, and interaction design.

- *User-experience assessment.* In addition to usability testing (formative and evaluative, and both in-lab and in the context of use) and heuristic analysis, activities in this category may involve the use of automated tools, such as click-stream analysis tools, that support analyses of general user behaviour patters. It also includes post-implementation activities, like log-file analysis, and working with client support and technical groups to identify ways of further enhancing user experiences.

XMod techniques, as the list suggests, derive from social science, market research and human-computer interaction. XMod is also evolving new approaches that will provide user experience insight that will be useful and valuable to clients and internal IntElegant teams.

User-Centred Design: the Internet Raises the Stakes

XMod's CXO observes that the Internet "raises the stakes" for user-centred design. "To manage complexity, we use a lot of socially constructed systems. I think the next big phase of user-centred design is giving people access to and confidence in those systems."

An example might be someone looking for medical information on the Internet. "In early interface design, what we worried about was how to do good searches, or how we organized what we retrieved. But what happens when we start to design for confidence in a diagnosis, or access to the entire system or network of treatment possibilities? When someone has as their access point to medical advice the global total of medical knowledge or medical infrastructure, instead of their physician, their point of experience is not a screen or a person, but the whole system; how to make that person feel comfortable with, or confident in, the whole system is a huge challenge. But I think that's what the Internet's given us."

In the Information Age, the stuff and staff of life is information. The digital revolution that began in the late twentieth century accelerates into the twenty-first: Computing becomes invisible, ubiquitous; your connection to the ÜberNet is always-already on. Pudgy broadband, skinny wireless. Artificial intelligence, bots, agents, avatars. User-interfaces: spoken, haptic, hedonic, kinetic, graphic, biologic. Don't let me forget cell phones. In this environment, an "affordable experience" isn't just something you may have enough money for. User-experience insight can be used for fun and profit. Companies can discover/invent/design new experiences and offer – afford – them to people.

The XMod vision offers insight to IntElegant's clients about their users; that leads to better products, branding, strategy, and profits. The vision also promises richer, more engaging user experiences. And the XMod vision helps IntElegant differentiate itself. Differentiate how? "By developing for our clients the best possible ability to understand and leverage experience for business strategy, and for the products and services or other solutions that matter to our clients' consumers and customers. We want to make people, our clients, and our colleagues understand that experience matters; that everyday experience, whether in the business context or in the consumer context, is where decisions that impact our clients" businesses are made, over and over again. It benefits our clients' bottom line to understand those experiences and to be able to use what they understand in the service of meaningful value propositions and offering development," answers IntElegant's VP of Experience (XVP), also an En Vivo alumna.

Despite the dot-com downturn IntElegant plans to build the discipline of user experience modelling. Says the CXO, "We've reached the point where it is so central to our message that we will continue to develop both message and method. We're starting to see clients explicitly mention XMod, or the specific insights and value that XMod work provides, as one of the reasons they've chosen IntElegant over competitors. Companies that haven't integrated this work into their central value proposition will think of this as expendable or marginal, and when times are tight, neither develop nor focus on it."

Defining and Designing "User Experience"

"What seems to be missing is a clear idea about what experience is; what its components or elements are; and, perhaps more importantly, whether it even can be designed or scripted," said Jody Forlizzi at a Usability Professionals' Association conference workshop on experience-based design (EBD) a couple of years ago.

XMod's view is that experience is both definable and designable. In the Fall 1998 issue of *The Journal of Design Management* an article appeared on experience-based design written by another En Vivo co-founder. EBD involves analysing everyday experience, and making the results useful to design stakeholders. It calls for creating an experience "framework," using ethnographic techniques to study what people "think, do, and use," gain insight into consumer experiences and identify opportunities for new and better ones.

The author is not aware of any ISO standard defining "user experience"; so what is it? XMod's XVP says: "We use 'experience' to refer to the ways in which people develop habits, assumptions, and routines in a particular domain. We do not believe our clients can or should in most cases be focused on the single event – experience is a repeated event and this means that it implies a history that is invoked each time an individual interacts with the particular product, interface or environment in question."

And Now . . . Whither XMod?

Susan Dray and David Siegel observed difficulties between promoting a vision and implementing the changes it requires. They acknowledge that a vision must be behind any company's effort to become more user-centred, but note that "Vision can get in the way of change when corporate activities that focus on vision are disconnected from the current work in progress. . . . By itself, a vision does not tell you what to do next." They also write that "despite the growing awareness of such things as the importance of good user interface (UI) design, usability, and UCD practices, it is extremely rare that companies adopt a fully integrated UCD approach in one grand strategic shift."

Written a year before XMod came into being, Dray and Siegel's observations seem relevant to XMod's first year. It hasn't been painless. Much of the emphasis in the discipline in the first months of its existence was on strategy rather than human-centred design. The nascent discipline seems to have gone through a bit of an identity crisis. There has been some confusion, for example, about what XMod is and what it does. "The notion of 'user experience' has become overexposed. It's moving toward becoming a mere buzzy sentiment," said one information architect. "I think there is a need for clarity. We need a nice, hard-edged conceptual model of XMod."

Lessons Learned

Though in its first year XMod may not have attained the Zen of Seamlessness, the goal is in view. In recent months, there has been a lot of progress toward strengthening human-centred design capabilities, for example, and attempts have been made to define the elusive "hard-edged conceptual model" of user experience. This is in tune with the key lessons learned during XMod's growth as a pioneering user experience modelling group:

- *A vision can hinder, as well as help:* A vision for user-centrism is necessary but the vision can interfere with change if it is disconnected from the current work in progress (or is perceived that way). Though IntElegant looks toward its e-business-strategy services having a larger role, much of the emphasis in the discipline in the first months of its existence was on strategy rather than human-centred design – thus the majority of the company's work remains the design and development of commercial and corporate web properties.

- *The building of a user experience modelling group must include the input of usability experts:* In IntElegant's legacy user-research group, XMod had considerable expertise in human-centred design and in introducing HCD into organizations. However, legacy researchers were not significantly involved in the building of their own discipline, which, as a result, tended far to much towards an ethnographic / strategy capability. This diminished the role of usability in an area where it should have been central. Morale among legacy IntElegant user researchers would have been better had they been more involved from the outset.

77

- *Understanding the "user experience" requires new tools and techniques:* A discipline-wide HCD initiative is afoot to train XModelers in HCD techniques, and educate project managers, directors and sales people about HCD. XMod has also begun to use automated tools that allow it to gather data about online behaviour. Says the CXO: "I think there's lots of tactical things we could get better at. They are certainly new tools emerging for understanding experience on the web where it's hard to be there in person; way beyond log analysis."

- *A new discipline will grow faster and establish itself more firmly if it is well understood at the executive level:* As Donald Norman pointed out, "[T]he real important decisions are, indeed, made at the top. Those are the people who will decide what direction you're moving in, what the time frame is, what the budget will be, where the emphasis is . . . and we need more people from the CHI community to be those executives . . . to be making those decisions which will eventually empower this profession. . . . [T]his field should not be about usability. . . . This field should be about empowering users, and that decision is made at the executive level."

The process of developing user experience modelling into a defined and useful discipline has taken time and effort, and is not yet complete at XMod. XMod's XVP concludes: "This past year has been a first step in starting to slowly shed the skin of where we come from. The En Vivo group has had to recognise that it's going to be more challenging than we all thought to figure out what we need to keep and what we need to get rid of so that we can work productively within the context that we're a part of now. . . . [W]e need to rethink how to best translate what was of real value to the methodology into this particular context. We are going to be doing an incredible amount of reinvention over the next few years."

References

Cain J (1998) "Toward a Science of Artful Business Innovation," The Journal of Design Management 9(4):Fall 1998

Dray S and Siegel D (1998) "User-Centred Design and the 'Vision Thing,'" interactions, March/April 1998, p. 16–17

Forlizzi J, www.goodgestreet.com/experience/rep99.html

Hammer B (2001) "'IntElegant' Cuts 720 Jobs – and Its Estimates," The Industry Standard, 2 March 2001, http://www.thestandard.com/article/display/0,1151,22596,00.html

Norman D (2000) "Organizational Limits to HCI: Conversations with Don Norman and Janice Rohn," Richard Anderson (ed.) interactions, May–June 2000, p. 39

Editor's Note

On 2 March 2001, between the completion of this chapter and the publication of this book, IntElegant laid off 720 people including some XModelers, approximately 20 per cent of its workforce. The company hopes to save $60–$65 million in the next year from the layoffs. Cuts were made across the board, in all disciplines, at all levels. At the time of writing there are no plans to disband XMod. George M Donahue no longer works for IntElegant.

Prototypes and Archetypes: Coping with Adult Behaviour in the Development of Information Systems for Children

8

Mike Pringle

The developmental lifecycle of a novel and untried human-computer inter-face, from drawing board conception to real-world implementation, is always likely to encounter, and often encourage, internal political debate. This chapter addresses, through reference to a user-centred, virtual reality based, project within English Heritage (EH), some of the human, technolog-ical and economic concerns that often arise within such debate. The chapter discusses the early requirement to secure internal sponsorship, or owner-ship, of the project, in an organization with little previous experience of user-centred HCI issues. It then traces progress through to the, perhaps surprising, situation of too many potential owners, the number of whom grew as understanding of usability and wider acceptance of the project's potential became apparent. The chapter focuses on several of the perceived, and real, problems that the project encountered; and illustrates how, through prototype demonstrations, technological reassurances, and consis-tent reiteration of the targeted users' viewpoint, the project responded to each of these challenges. Discussing the development process of the PastScape project, Chapter 8 illustrates some of the ways EH has been addressing the pervasive, and sometimes intrusive growth of Information Communication Technologies (ICT). In particular, this chapter refers to several usability issues that the project's novel nature raised, and to a number of approaches taken in establishing the resulting system within the organization, as a viable and potentially valuable tool.

Introduction and Background

English Heritage is a national organization with primary tasks relating to the guardianship and management of archaeological and historical sites, monuments and buildings in England; EH is also responsible, particularly since 1999 when it merged with the Royal Commission on the Historic Monuments of England (RCHME), for the collection, curation and dissemination of huge quantities of heritage information. Information in the form of data-sets, drawings and photographs, covering a substantial range of subject matters for a large and diverse target audience.

In order to address some of the political usability issues within EH, this chapter focuses on one particular project, part of a one-year research and development programme, based on research which RCHME had been involved in for several years previously. The project, with the working title of PastScape, revolved around the design and development of a prototype computer system which, if implemented, would present heritage information (from English Heritage's National Monuments Record database) to an imaginary "intelligent 12-year-old" audience via a novel and highly intuitive, Internet-based interface. Children, and non-expert adults, would be able to navigate, in an enjoyable way, a collection of user-friendly virtual reality (VR) models, representing monument types, time periods and English counties. A prototype was constructed, for demonstration purposes, featuring VR models, developed using Superscape's SVR format, within an HTML and JavaScript template and combined with text, images and hyper-text links. The HCI was designed to send queries to an underlying Oracle dataset, in response to user decisions, and return HTML pages relating explicitly to the areas of expressed user-interest.

Politics of Persuasion: The Use of Prototyping to Engender Ownership

The PastScape project was born as part of a response to the great changes, in the way ICT is increasingly being used and viewed, that have occurred recently in all areas of modern western society. When the idea of a novel ICT project was first conceived in 1996, the Internet, World Wide Web (the web), VR and other seemingly sophisticated technologies, were still something of a novelty to many people in many British workplaces. Despite this, there was definitely an optimistic air, and the potential of the new technologies was acknowledged by a commitment, initially from RCHME, and then EH, to explore the possibilities through the design and construction of an experimental, almost fully-functional, prototype. Thus the PastScape project began.

Although generalizing, it is probably reasonable to speculate that the heritage sector, particularly where concerned with ICT, has a fair share of intelligent, and highly committed people. Also, the nature of heritage, concerned as it is with many complex cultural, sociological, and even scientific issues, tends naturally to create an environment of investigation that is neither satisfied, nor fooled, by superficial or arbitrary solutions. The project began at a time when much ICT, and particularly the web and VR, were in a state of some immaturity, and it is always difficult to convince people to invest time, money and staff into something as ill-defined as the future of such technologies. This is especially true of a project proposing to explore new HCI ideas and approaches, instead of adhering to notions that are already proven, or that can be seen to be developing positively elsewhere. In fact, one of the overriding priorities of the project was to see if high levels of usability could be achieved through methods that deliberately differed from previous RCHME and EH systems (which were predominantly designed for internal and professional use), and also diverged from the most commonly used approaches emerging, at that time, on the web. Consequently, the project's success relied on ensuring that an area of the business took ownership of the resulting system, and this was only likely to happen if EH personnel could be persuaded that the various novel elements of the interface could add value to the business. The following sections outline some of the issues, that such a course of action will often encounter, and focus on approaches used in the project to persuade rational, intelligent adults of several of the sometimes unclear benefits of usability.

Fitness Exercises: the Importance of Recognizing Underlying Perceptions

Every software developer, HCI designer or usability specialist is aware of the importance of making any system appropriate, or fit, for its intended purpose; and that the intended purpose of any system is ultimately that which the end-user wants or needs to do with it. On this basis, and before the PastScape project itself was born, a bespoke requirements-capture method was devised, incorporating several well-known analysis and survey techniques. The aim of this exercise was to try and identify useful and practical mappings between the business needs (problem domain), and the techno-logical hardware, software and processes that were, or soon would be, available to the organization (solution domain). Although there was an expressed intention to develop a novel ICT application, and a desire to make use of VR and Internet technologies, at this early stage no specific thoughts were formulated about what shape any resulting project would take, nor to what end. Instead, the research method was designed to establish whether or not there were any business areas that could, at that time, benefit from the implementation of new ICT systems or approaches.

From the outset the pre-developmental research involved considerable consultation with a wide variety of staff, including senior personnel (direc-tors), IS (Information Systems) staff, as well as specialists and users in other areas of the corporate structure. The input provided by such a variety of people, and their very different perspectives, inevitably proved to be extremely useful, and enabled a comprehensive and realistic overview of the organization to be established. The output included plans, descriptions, flow-diagrams and discussions of all of the organization's major functions; IT capabilities; divisions and departments; external partners; financial restraints; and its corporate and strategic visions for the future. The investi-gation was helped by the fact that, because this was effectively blue sky research, there were few negative pre-conceptions associated with it, and thus staff involvement in the early stages was fairly spontaneous and enthu-siastic. The perceived potential, offered by the very latest innovations in technologies such as the web and VR, was great, and certainly worth a degree of investment in both time and effort.

There was also, however, a flip side to this particular coin. As a consequence of the fact that the project began with a clean sheet, and because the initial analysis focused on an examination of business functions, it was difficult to explain to those involved what it was that was being asked of them; inter-viewed staff, understandably, wanted an idea of what was to be developed so that they could temper their responses accordingly. Intuitively, they were trying to ensure that their input was itself "fit for purpose". This led to a degree of uncertainty that seemed to be counteracted by "playing safe", i.e. responses tended to be high-level, in accord, particularly, with the deliver-ables of an organization-wide IS strategy study that had been completed only a matter of months earlier. Whilst this may still have produced a fair overview of the IS elements of the organization, it meant that some "reading between the lines" was necessary to identify areas that could benefit from new technological systems, approaches or ideas; quite reasonably, no one wanted to consider the possibility of areas that "could do better", especially after so much time, money and effort had so recently been put into a substantial IS study. Furthermore, although the staff respondents were enthusiastic and helpful during the analysis process, finding someone to take firm internal ownership of the project, a "champion", proved to be a difficult task. Retrospectively this seems fairly predictable because, during the early stages, no one had the faintest idea what it was they would be championing!

Fortunately, belief in a positive outcome, combined with the continued help and goodwill of staff (including some with enough faith to take at least limited ownership), enabled the process to continue. Ultimately, the research method revealed a commitment to increase the dissemination of heritage information, stored predominantly in computer databases. It also revealed that, due to various constraints, this commitment was not being addressed as quickly as the organization wanted. Combining this factor with the earlier intentions to make use of VR and Internet technologies, it was decided to try to develop a system that would allow users to explore heritage data, via VR models, on the web. The only missing factor seemed to be who exactly these mysterious, obliging, "users" were!

Expressing the Role of the User by Creating an Archetypal Character

Identifying an average user of the Internet, is at best implausible, and, more probably, impossible; but this does not exonerate systems designers from trying. The previous section described how a research method was devised to establish purpose, for the design of a novel IS, but mentioned at the outset how it is the wants or needs of the end-user that must always be the overriding purpose of any such system. Consequently, the method, although sufficient for ensuring compatibility between system and organization, was not enough to *guarantee* end-user satisfaction. As work began on prototype development, it became apparent that identification of end-users of the system needed further clarification.

Discussion revealed that the organization had very clear perspectives on some members of the public that take an interest in the heritage. They could be described as those that already made use of its services, its *current* customer base, and a very concrete understanding of their needs and wants already existed. Accordingly, there was a feeling that the customer, or potential user, was already known, and did not therefore need to be discovered, nor included in either development or system-testing. However, because the PastScape project was exploring an untapped area, its resulting application had the potential to reach a whole *new* customer base, customers whose identities were not yet discovered. Although internal belief and external reality may have been a perfect match, there was no evidence to assert this possibility, and without a concrete external user to target, the system risked only satisfying an internalized viewpoint, without necessarily improving the organization's dissemination of information. Furthermore, there is always a danger, with such an internalised viewpoint, that the wrong emphasis can be placed on decisions; for example, regarding which particular dataset should take advantage of a new, and potentially advantageous, system.

Many organizations are structured in such a way that different sections, divisions or departments have responsibility, and therefore ownership, for different elements of the organization's data. This carries with it the possibility that a dataset will be chosen according to some sort of purely internal motivation, rather than for the benefit of an intended user. In an attempt to resolve this issue satisfactorily, i.e. to promote wider internal acceptance of the principles of user-centred design, two different approaches were established. The first was to compose a "typical" user; the second was to explain the correlation between the potential new system and certain current business practices. These two approaches are outlined here:

The Intelligent 12-year-old

Because the perfect typical, or average, user does not, unfortunately, exist, early usability experiments for this project were conducted with the involvement of a variety of potential user-group representatives. The test-subject volunteer force (some 48 people, half of whom were males, and the other half, females) was composed of equal ratios of: heritage professionals; computer experts; lay people with no expertise in either heritage or computing; and, children aged between 9 and 11 years. However, in everyday discussions with EH staff it was impractical, to say the least, to try and explain that every element of the system was being designed to disseminate information to this convoluted cross section of society. Thus, all four types, and both genders, became assimilated into a single, easily explained, "intelligent 12-year-old". From the moment that this creation took life, explaining or rationalising any element of the system, to almost anyone, took on a new and surprising simplicity and clarity. Most people seemed to naturally understand what was meant by an intelligent 12-year-old, had no problem seeing why such a character had arisen from our collection of test subjects, and, perhaps most interestingly, accepted that such a persona was appropriate, as an "average" user of the Internet with a possible interest in heritage matters.

From Data to Information

The second approach taken, to demonstrate the importance of a target audience, was to clarify the functionality of a usable system by relating it to more easily recognised, non-IS, business functions. It was necessary, at various stages, to attain approval from people within EH who were well acquainted with dealing with the public, and whose natural responses revolved around familiar business processes, usually from a non-IT viewpoint, but often with an informed knowledge of web or IS principles. Drawing on the results of the initial analytical method, and through discussion with internal staff, a picture was revealed of some of the business practices that were already being used to disseminate database information to the public, and to other heritage professionals. The area of the organization's business structure that was most relevant to the project at that time, centred around EH's National Monuments Record Centre (NMRC) where members of the public could request heritage information. An enquiry would elicit a search by a team of in-house professionals, using various national databases and archives, and the results would be supplied to the enquirer. Essential to this process, which is of course an information system, are: the existence of data; an understanding of the data; an interpretation of the user's requirement; and delivery of appropriate information. Appropriate, of course, to the end-user. This, the process of turning data into information, is illustrated in *Fig. 8.1.* Within the NMRC, the in-house professionals perform this complex task by interpreting what the user wants, being able to understand the terminology and structure of the data, and then by presenting a suitable end-product.

Taking this already-understood process, or service to the user, and equating it to what a good IS should provide, was a useful ally in the explanation of the new interface, especially to those who were regular users of the Internet; many web-sites fail to provide this absolutely essential service, instead simply making raw data available. Such sites are not truly *information* systems, they are data storage systems with multiple-user access.

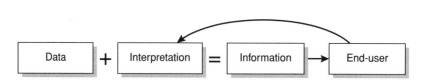

Figure 8.1 The simplified information process

Distinguishing Between Subjective and Objective Issues: What Exactly Does a Picture Paint?

Interpretation of data, to provide information, will always raise subjective issues. The very notion that information should be placed into a context that is "appropriate" for a user, confirms that different people will tend to interpret the same thing in different ways. Images are a good example of this: everybody knows that a picture paints a thousand words; the problem is that they can often be a different thousand words for each viewer! Computer graphics, without a doubt, convey a substantial quantity of information to the viewer, and, bandwidth issues aside, can be a very powerful component of any modern computer-based HCI, especially where there is an expressed desire to appeal to a younger audience (even if imaginary). As the support-gaining exercise continued, the PastScape project, with its considerable, and unorthodox graphical elements (in the form of simple VR models) both suffered and gained as a result of their inclusion.

Within the prototype model, graphics were used to illustrate complex abstract concepts such as time periods, geographical locations, and monument classes using the well established pictorial abstractions of time-lines and maps, and models representative of different monument types, such as Religious or Military. Use of such abstractions, when considered in the light of an intelligent 12-year-old, led naturally to the idea of developing the VR images in a similar vein to school-book diagrams, i.e. containing enough detail to elucidate the appropriate information, and presented in a clean, simple and brightly coloured style. This all seemed fine, but one or two flaws appeared in the plan as the end-products, in various states of preparation, were presented to more and more people. Archaeological content, and degree of accuracy, balanced against the need for simplicity, was the first issue with early versions of the VR illustrations being met with comments such as "monument X shouldn't have windows that shape!" or "monument Y doesn't belong to that period!".

These comments are of course not subjective, but educated. However, they were often followed by "I think you would be better off if you did . . .", and at this point we entered the realm of opinion. By having genuine flaws, the design process unwittingly invited in subjective criticism, which will always threaten to make development more complex than necessary. Resolution involved more research, and greater input from a restricted number of, firm but fair, expert individuals within the organization. Although any result of this new, collective, viewpoint would still be subjective, it would be tempered by various knowledgeable opinions, and thus be nearer to some sort of objective view. Having a defendable viewpoint, that was more likely to be shared by other heritage professionals, added more credibility to the project when questions were raised elsewhere in the support-gaining exercise. Furthermore, it meant that a significant part of the interface's content was now partially owned by an identifiable area of the business. Of course, bringing in more opinions increased the risk of an internalised viewpoint, but this was avoided by constant iterations involving staff, but keeping fitness of purpose (the intelligent 12-year-old) uppermost in all discussions.

Making extensive use of VR graphics in the prototype stimulated a second, double-sided, issue. The plus side was fairly obvious in its nature, but quite surprising in its potency; many people were (are) impressed by flashy, animated computer graphics. As Brooks advocates, graphics relate much more directly to the way humans naturally interpret and communicate information (Brooks, 1996), and this obviously effects the way people respond to a highly graphical interface. This is very useful for improving end-user perception, because if he/she finds interacting with the system a pleasurable, or fun, experience, then navigation and information gathering are more likely to be successful. It is also extremely useful in gaining approval for a new system! The perceived impressiveness of naturally-interactive and visually-stimulating graphics can win over all but the most hardened heart. Unfortunately, two disadvantages to using these graphics became apparent in the PastScape project, one relating to cost and the other to expectation.

VR modelling, with full three-dimensionality, extensive animation, and elaborate fly-throughs can be seen as a potential cost problem: cost in time and money; and, cost in download times and user-system requirements. These are, of course, the normal sort of issues that any such new business development must face; risk assessment questions must always be asked. PastScape's graphical components were fairly straightforward to quantify, since most questions relating to them were fielded either during or after demonstrations of the prototype, after much of the graphical content had already been completed without any undue strain on resources. The second issue, that of download times and user-system requirements, was more complex because VR modelling did indeed have some associated cost. Furthermore, EH had a commitment to a non-exclusion policy: it was, and still is, imperative that EH information should be made available to all, not just a select few who can afford, or get access to, the very latest computer tools. Consequently, and despite having the intelligent 12-year-old as a representative of a "typical" user, the range of potential levels of hardware and software availability across the user-base was huge, and thus the consideration of usability, in the interface design, had an unusually high level of significance. Dealing with these issues, in the course of trying to justify the PastScape structure, produced a single solution: multiple versions of the interface.

Many current web-sites are designed to work on some definition of a lowest common denominator; for example, it is very common to see sites that are designed to fill a 640 × 480 pixel resolution space. Unfortunately, such sites frequently look awkward on larger monitors, with a common occurrence being an excess of "white space" to the right of the actual content. Also, it is easy to forget that the sort of computer that has only a small monitor is likely to be a fairly low specification machine, possibly with a slow modem, and usually with an older graphics capability and a limited number of display colours. There are various graphic design solutions to these issues, and even the occasional technotrick to help, but the optimum solution, which has political implications, is hinted at in the problem itself. The only reason that an interface appears differently on different machines is because it is being viewed by *different* sorts of users, and the only solution is to provide *different* interfaces, appropriate to each sort. This may seem excessive, and this is where it can become political, because superficially the quantity of work required to provide this level of usability may be beyond normal expectations, and seem to have a cost implication. Nonetheless, the PastScape prototype was fortunate enough to be developed in a culture that accepted the need to be non-exclusive towards its vast and varied potential user-base, and the reality of producing different versions was soon shown to be perfectly feasible, and several interfaces were developed. Once the basic structure, graphics and textual content were established it took remarkably little effort to tweak the material into slightly varying versions for different screen resolutions, as well as a standard web-site version, and a text-only version.

Success, and What We Learned from It

The PastScape project was a one-year research programme involving the development of a prototype model, which was used to demonstrate the feasibility of some new HCI concepts and ideas, in order to justify a place for itself (and find an owner) within the organization. After numerous meetings, discussions, presentations and demonstrations, involving a considerable number of people, both internally and externally, it was decided that the system was both viable and potentially useful to EH's future ICT plans. Accordingly, the project was elevated from research programme to business project status with a view to implementing a fully-functional version at some future time.

This success can be attributed, from a usability point of view, to a simple user-centred philosophy that was applied not only to the end-user, but also to the people involved within the encompassing business. Demonstrations or presentations to staff, of each aspect of the system, were treated as the delivery of information to an end-user, with each being structured according to who was in the audience. Slowly, and through trying to understand objections (as well as not being lured too far by praise!), the presentations became more and more in tune with the needs of EH, and consequently it became easier to explain, and gain acceptance for the novel usability factors that were demonstrated in the prototype. This chapter has outlined several perfectly reasonable issues, raised as a consequence of discussions with EH staff, that the project faced , and described some of the approaches used to deal with them. These can be summed up in the following way:

Understand the Importance of Initial Staff Perceptions

Pre-development research is obviously imperative, but it is important to remember that it is not just the researcher who will need to establish "fitness of purpose"" the subjects on the receiving end of any research interview (interrogation?) will want, and need, to understand exactly what it is that is required from them in order to respond in a way that ensures realistic and honest results.

Find Ways to Describe an "Archetypal User"

Where the end-user is ill-defined, or includes more than a single type of person, a compromise, or assimilated "archetypal" user can be created. In the PastScape project, the intelligent 12-year-old proved an invaluable asset in explaining, and sometimes justifying, many aspects of the system.

Explain the System-to-User-Process

IS functionality is primarily concerned with a service to the user, whereby business-owned data is processed into usable information. It is useful, in trying to gain internal support for a new system, to make positive comparisons between how the system will deliver this service, and, already understood business functions, particularly those relating to the jobs that "real" people do.

Manage the Trade-Off Between Objectivity and Subjectivity

Any of the visible elements of an interface; for example, graphics, may engender subjective opinion from many viewpoints. Associated risks can be diluted by identifying, and inviting on board, a restricted number of experts (who are acknowledged as such within the organization), and thus give added credibility to the system itself. Graphics are useful in adding a degree of fun for the user, and through their inherent, but subjectively, user-friendly feel, can help to persuade people of the potency of a system. However, it is very easy to be blinded by these benefits (as user, customer or designer), and to ensure that different user requirements are met it is desirable to provide a variety of interface versions, including; for example, a text-only version.

And Finally . . .

This chapter has discussed a few of the HCI issues that the PastScape project met in attaining corporate ownership, and has described some of the lessons learned that were useful in justifying novel usability features. Success in any attempt to increase understanding, or acceptance of usability, ulti- mately requires an understanding or acceptance on the part of the usability promoter, of the sort of reactions that are likely to be encountered. We, as such promoters, must always bear in mind that the behaviour of our "customers" is invariably adult, and thus rational and sensible in nature; and, if acceptance is to be forthcoming, must be met with an equally adult, respectful approach.

Gaining acceptance for the system, and its novel usability factors, was obvi- ously a central aim of the PastScape project, and, substantially because of an increased understanding of the importance of usability, the project's princi- ples were indeed accepted throughout the organization. As a consequence more and more suggested application-areas emerged, and peculiar though it may seem, this success led to another political question: which area of the business would own the real-world system? Fortunately this is not a usability issue!

Reference

Brooks F (1996) The Computer Scientist as Toolsmith, Communications of the ACM, 39(3)

Prototypes in Web-Site Design – Representations with Political Agenda

9

Nick Bryan-Kinns, Magnus Lif, Fraser Hamilton
and Ismail Ismail

Throughout the design of an e-business site, a variety of representations are used to communicate design ideas between different stakeholders – clients, users, graphic designers, software developers, etc. These representations range from hand drawn sketches through to working web pages and are developed using a variety of tools. In this chapter we present two case studies of the use of such representations in the design of interactive web pages for large multinational companies. In particular, we consider the politics of different stakeholders' use of such representations. We follow this through by elucidating the lessons we have learnt from this experience, and moreover, how we and others working in web-site usability might use such representations in the future.

Introduction

Icon Medialab creates, designs and builds e-commerce web-sites. In order to achieve this, several different skill competencies work together to develop sites, e.g. usability engineering, graphic design, coding, and management consulting. This necessarily involves much communication between the competencies. As in other joint ventures, we use, and rely on, representations to help communicate ideas, concepts, and routes to realization. One class of representations are prototypes. Much research and work experience has demonstrated the utility of a prototype driven approach, particularly when developing interactive systems in an iterative manner.

For example, Boehm (1988) claims that the conventional software development model (referred to as the waterfall model) is not suitable when developing interactive systems. Such approaches may lead to problems such as inaccurate understanding of user needs, software that is hard to maintain or extend, late discovery of serious project flaws, and an inability to deal with changing requirements (Krutchen, 2000). As a solution, Boehm suggests a spiral model of development where analysis, design and evaluation are performed in an iterative way, relying on various representations. Problems ... be discovered early in the process, making it easier ... istakes and make changes. However, to make this ... the time for each iteration has to be short. In most ... e and money set hard limits.

... d, iterative development approaches when devel- ... ototypes can show navigation structure, content, ... aspects of the user interface. As we shall see ... choice of which aspects of the interaction are ... ypes, as well as how they are presented and ... acts on the development.

... ototypes in Use

... ed in this chapter we have identified three main ... ig. 9.1) which impact on the use of prototypes ... which they are used. Given that these dimen- ... rojects discussed in this chapter, they are very ... ns of what we believe to influence the politics ... at is, we have used them to reason about and to ... the projects. For clarity, then, we present the ... e case studies to provide reference points to ... rld situations in which prototypes have caused

... lelity of the prototype. This ranges from hand ... ugh to fully interactive computer based repre- ... et audience is considered. This ranges from ... eers, across various disciplines within the ... signers and coders, through to external partic- ... as clients. Third, we consider the stage of development at which the prototype is used. In a classical waterfall model this ranges from requirements analysis through to testing. We do not constrain ourselves by the simple linear waterfall model of development, but use the stages identified

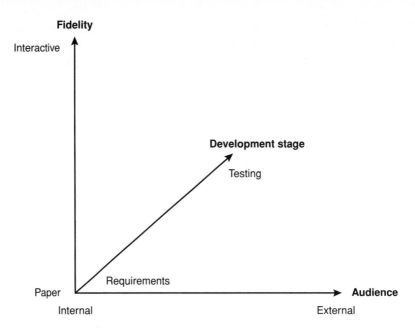

Figure 9.1 Prototypes vary along three dimensions: audience, fidelity and development stage

as a way of understanding the target audience and purpose of the prototype. We typically employ a spiral approach where initial requirements are captured, prototypes are developed and tested, results of which feed in to more detailed requirements analysis. This iterative approach continues until we have a concrete set of requirements and prototypes which are used to drive actual development in parallel with further usability testing.

The Case Studies

In this section we discuss our experiences of using prototypes to develop e-commerce solutions for two large multinational companies referred to as A and B. In project A we were asked to build an e-commerce site from scratch; all aspects of the project were to be undertaken in-house (or by subcontracting), but using "out-of-the-box" e-commerce back-end systems. In project B we were asked to redesign an existing site. The main reason was that the site was lacking in consistency because functionality and features had been added over a long period of time and lacked focus. A key aim was to build a stable and flexible technical architecture to enable easy maintenance and future proof. In this project the user interface design and software development were done in-house while the graphic design was done by another company.

Overview of Project A

In Project A we started by eliciting users' requirements through a series of workshops with users and clients and through reviews of competitors' sites. These lead to an understanding of the basic strategies users might employ in purchasing their consumer goods on-line. We used these requirements and our understandings of the domain to inform the design of several different paper prototypes over a period of a week (e.g. the anonymized paper proto-type shown in *Fig. 9.2*). The key purpose of the paper prototype was to establish the overall navigation and content structure of the site. These paper prototypes were designed and viewed only by the usability engineers: at this early stage our ideas were not communicated to other members of the design team or client.

Once we were happy with the usability of the paper prototype we started to develop a prototype referred to as a wireframe – a set of web pages which would map to final web pages, but with limited functionality and graphic design (e.g. the anonymized wireframe shown in *Fig. 9.3*). These wireframes were of a higher fidelity than the paper prototypes, demonstrating more functionality, dynamic navigation and having example content in the form of products and text. The wireframes were designed to serve two basic

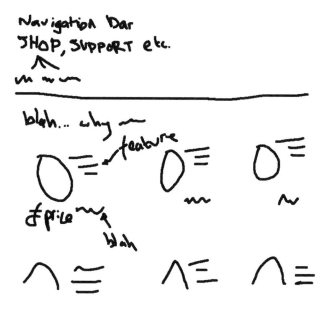

Figure 9.2 Anonymized paper prototype

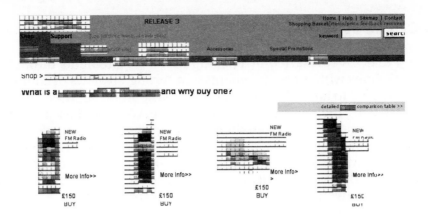

Figure 9.3 Anonymized wireframe

purposes: first, to show the navigation and the basic page set required for the site to other team members and the client; second, to be used in user testing prior to the start of implementation.

Overview of Project B

The aim of Project B was to redesign an existing site which had evolved over time and had become inconsistent. As with Project A, we went through a number of workshops with the client to identify their aims with the site and to get a better understanding of the brand and users' needs. We also analysed competitors' sites and their own market research to find out more about client B's target audience and their relationship with the client's brand and products. Additionally we involved around 250 users in a questionnaire study to complement the clients' own research.

Following this research, we developed low-fidelity paper prototypes (similar to those used in Project A) to visualize ideas on how products and information could be represented on the site. The paper prototypes also helped us identify gaps and to highlight issues that needed to be resolved.

As with Project A, when the paper prototype was "finished" we started to build a higher-fidelity wireframe. The wireframe was a first step towards an interactive prototype representing the main scenarios of the site. Again, the intention with the wireframe was not to illustrate the "look" of the site, but rather to demonstrate the flow and the information architecture without restricting the graphic design.

In both Projects A and B, then, the development of the user interface followed similar paths. After conducting user, market and brand research, paper prototypes were developed. These paper prototypes were used solely within the HCI team to reason about information structure, content and navigation. The paper prototyping was followed in both cases with the development of an interactive wireframe for a wider audience including HCI people, graphic designers, coders, the client and users. As we shall see in the rest of this section, however, supporting this wide range of audiences led to fidelity and version tensions within the prototype as well as political tensions between audiences as development continued.

Political Tensions in Projects A and B

Communication with Clients

One of the first political stumbling blocks we encountered with our wireframes in project A was their use in client discussions. Our aim in initial client meetings was to arrive at agreement about how the site would work in terms of navigation, and the kinds of content for each page such as photos, text, tables and so on. However, because of the apparently realistic content and dynamic behaviour, the client tended to focus on small details of content rather than broad views of the navigational and content structure – the very aspects on which we wanted feedback. For example, we put fictional prices with their products, and used fictional attributes to illustrate how real attributes would be displayed. While this approach saves time in developing prototypes, as real values do not have to be researched, the client latched on to these specific parts of the prototype asking questions such as "do we really sell them at that price" and "I didn't realize that product came in that colour". Constantly explaining the rough nature of the prototype meant that we concentrated on small details rather than discussing the overall nature of the proposed web-site.

In terms of our dimensions we would suggest that at this early stage of our ideas the prototype was too high in fidelity for the target audience (the clients). In retrospect, it would have been better to use rougher prototypes at this stage with the client, e.g. paper prototypes, or clickable paper-looking prototypes using a computer to show the navigational flow.

In Project B the wireframe worked relatively well as a communication tool with the client. It made it relatively easy to explain and discuss ideas of information structure and functionality with the client as the wire frame made it very concrete. The problem with the wireframe in Project B was that the client thought the wire frame was close to the final site but for us it was not. This led to problems when communicated to the external graphic design agency (see Communicating with Graphic Designers). We had different interpretations of the fidelity of the wireframe which led to political tensions.

Communication with Coders

In contrast to the wireframe being overly defined for the clients when discussing overall structure of the site in Project A, we found that compositional elements of pages were not defined in sufficient detail to communicate with the software development team responsible for implementation. The development teams' approach was to identify logical units within each page so that common software classes and routines could be identified early on. This entailed marking up the prototypes with regions regarded as logical units, and numbering them (see *Fig. 9.4* as an annotated version of *Fig. 9.3*). Clearly this added another level of detail to the wireframe which we had not initially envisioned when designing it. Since the wireframe was developed in HTML using layers it was not technically possible to annotate the prototype itself, so paper copies of the pages were used and marked up. As development progressed, and the prototype was refined due to client requests and an improved understanding of the user requirements, it became increasingly difficult to maintain a link between the regions marked on the paper copies and the evolving prototype.

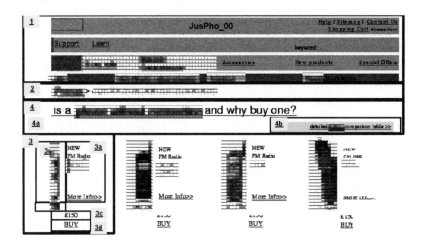

Figure 9.4 Anonymized annotated wireframe

Given the lack of fidelity in the prototype required by the software coders, use cases were written to specify the user-system interaction in more detail. Use cases are a software development representation that describes the "dialogue" between a user and system in a task context. For example, in the task context of "Write an e-mail", the dialogue could be: (1) The user creates a new message; (2) The system displays an empty message window; (3) The user gets a recipient from the address book; (4) The system checks the validity of the address, and so on. These use cases were specified by use-case writers and then taken by a test team who developed test plans to better support the implementation effort. These additional specifications referred directly to particular parts of the wireframe – for example, the use cases detailed particular user-system interactions, while the test plans relied on both the wireframes and use cases. Maintaining the consistency between these multiple representations became more difficult as more and more people came to rely on the wireframe.

In terms of our dimensions, our prototype did not allow for sufficient detail in its description when the target audience was the software development team. Moreover, the unchanging paper copies became further out of synch with the evolving prototype as development progressed thus imposing an overhead on the communication between the HCI and development teams. Essentially the development team needed a view of the prototype that was at a greater level of detail than our own.

The same problem occurred again in Project B where the prototype was used as a means of communication between the HCI team and the software coders. As in Project A the prototype was not detailed enough to meet the needs of the coders. Therefore we adopted use cases to further detail the requirements on the functionality. Initially HCI was responsible for specifying the use cases. However, at a later stage the system developers took on this responsibility to make sure the use cases were detailed enough to support them in their work. The use cases together with the wire frame were used to drive the development process and to identify issues that needed to be resolved.

Communicating with Users

In project A the development team wanted each item of each page to be more thoroughly defined than in our wireframes. This is essentially fidelity in terms of describing what each element does, where its data comes from, what constraints are placed on it, etc. We found that the prototype was lacking a different kind of fidelity when conducting user tests of the navigational structure of the prototype. In this situation we asked users to perform various tasks that the site was designed to support. However, the visual appearance of the wireframes (i.e. no graphic design) tended to distract the users from their tasks. This is in some ways similar to the situation in which the client for Project A was distracted by the arbitrary content used in the wireframes, but in this case the arbitrary visual design of the wireframes caused the distraction. Thus, while the wireframe more or less behaved like a web-site and the content appeared realistic, the visual appearance was perhaps too under-specified to provide for a completely coherent user experience. A lesson here is that the fidelity of the prototype should be consistent in terms of its content, navigation, functionality and visual design for optimal user testing.

This is in contrast to the user testing in Project B. The web-site in Project B was developed and delivered within extremely tight deadlines to meet seasonal demands in the marketplace. In Project B the site was evaluated later in the lifecycle when the graphic design was complete and integrated with the functionality. In this case, user feedback and problems related to the fact that users identified a gap between their interpretation of the off-line brand and the representation of the brand on the site. Unlike in Project A, the users were not distracted by inconsistencies between the content, navigation, and visual design. Of course, in both projects the usability evaluations nonetheless proved extremely valuable and guided us in making changes prior to launch.

The lesson here appears to be that users, as an audience of prototypes, prefer using systems that are consistent along the fidelity dimension. That is, we tentatively suggest that user testing is perhaps most effective when the content, navigation, behaviour, functionality and visual appearance are at similar levels of completion or realism. When this is not the case, users may become distracted from their tasks.

Communicating with Graphic Designers

Of course, the prototypes we develop are an indispensable part of the development process without which we, as usability engineers, would have serious trouble developing usable e-commerce sites. We found (unsurprisingly) that it was most appropriate for use within the HCI group (so the target audience was ourselves): we have shared concerns, terminology, education and so on. However, unlike the development team (coders, use case writers, etc.), we found that the graphic design group were able to use our wireframes with minimal explanation required on our part. We believe that this was due to a close match between our and their requirements – we defined what elements should be on each page, and what groupings would be appropriate which was precisely the starting point that they needed.

However, we saw a different situation in Project B in which the graphic design of the site was not done in-house but was out-sourced by the client to another company. When all stakeholders were satisfied with the wireframe it was "frozen". The client then used it to communicate what services and information should be on the site to the out-sourced graphic designers. We were not really involved in this communication. The client had asked the graphic design company to "colour in" the wireframe without making any changes to the flow or the interactivity. This was something that we had not foreseen and were unhappy about. The intention with the wireframe was never to act simply as a template to be coloured in, but as a vehicle for communicating basic flow and information structure. While the issues arising out of this misunderstanding were resolved, the outsourcing of the graphics work made for difficulties in communicating between the HCI and graphic design team. In this situation we see that our intention behind the fidelity of the prototype (low) was not conveyed to the target audience (the graphic designers) who perceived it to be finished. This resulted in political tension between ourselves, our client, and the graphic design company.

In terms of our dimensions, it appears that graphic designers, as "consumers" of prototypes, share similar concerns as usability engineers in that both groups are focussed on the user experience. Moreover, the output of HCI work as wireframes, at least within our company, is an ideal starting point for graphic design work. However, while two competencies working within the same company may share this understanding and co-ordination, it is clear that this may not be the case when a third party is brought into the project. Obviously, good working relationships depend on a shared under-standing and co-ordination of activities. The communication necessary for such understanding and co-ordination may be facilitated or hampered by the nature of the representations used.

Conclusion

Throughout the discussion of our use of prototypes we have seen how they are a central component in the development of highly interactive e-commerce solutions. From a usability point of view it is difficult to see how usable systems can be developed without them. HCI as a discipline woefully lacks predictive or prescriptive principles that designers can apply to guarantee usability, and so prototyping and user testing must go hand-in-hand (Hamilton et al., 1998). Even if such principles did exist, prototypes nonetheless are invaluable for sharing design intentions with other usability experts, clients, users, coders, graphic designs, and so on. Successful projects rely on these stakeholders having a shared understanding of the design space and effectively coordinating their activities. We have seen how prototypes can help or hinder this shared understanding and coordination: we have seen how clients can focus on details of content while designers want to discuss the general content structure and navigation. Coders require more detail than can be embodied in the early stages of design. Yet graphic designers can use prototypes as an ideal starting point for their work. Even though our primary aim in each of the two case studies discussed was to develop prototypes suitable for user-testing, the other stakeholders nonetheless found it invaluable for understanding the envisaged solution. It is when the prototype inadequately supports this shared understanding or coordination that political tensions can arise. Like all representations, prototypes have a purpose, and using one prototype for different audiences with different concerns is inevitably going to hamper communication and coordination. We expand on these conclusions in the following section by outlining the lessons learnt.

Summary

Prototypes are an invaluable resource in modern system development as a means of communicating design ideas to a wide variety of audiences. We have presented three dimensions pertinent to the use of prototypes: fidelity, audience and stage of product development. We illustrated the political issues that arise when the tensions between these dimensions arise. Finally, we considered our requirements for support of our work practices.

Our experiences led to extensive searches for suitable tools to support our work processes. What we really wanted was some sort of tool which would allow us to develop multifaceted prototypes to suit the needs of different audiences and phases of development. One tool that closely met our needs appeared to be Denim (Newman and Landay, 2000). It supports sketchy prototyping, linking prototype pages together, and offering different views of the prototype such as outline navigation structures. However, for our needs we also require the ability to link the pages to graphically designed versions as well as being able to attach descriptions of logical components. In addition we need support for change management and report generation (ideally, the automatic generation of use cases from scenarios).

Lessons Learnt

We have presented two case studies demonstrating how we use prototypes in developing e-commerce solutions. These prototypes were developed by usability engineers and used by a variety of audiences including users, clients, software developers, and graphic designers. We have attempted to demonstrate that these audiences had different concerns and thus needed different information out of the prototype. In this section, we reflect upon some of these findings and suggest ways to overcome the tensions we experienced. Two main lessons emerge from the case studies.

Lesson 1: Prototypes Serve a Purpose – They Are Not a "Jack of all Trades"

Our paper and interactive prototypes proved an invaluable representation around which development progressed. The main lesson that we learnt through the use of prototypes was that one prototype was simply inadequate for the whole development process and the different audiences involved. Specifically, the fidelity of the prototype needs to be aligned to the needs of a particular audience for the stage of development they find themselves in.

Attempting to use one prototype (i.e. one fidelity) for all audiences, in all stages, can lead to political tensions including:

- A lack of definition for software development (e.g. coders) during implementation.

- Too much definition for client overviews in the early stages of design.

- Low graphic design which confused users during evaluation.

- Misunderstood fidelity for out-sourced project members.

These political tensions can compound the problems, particularly during implementation phases, when additional specifications are developed to complement the prototypes. We especially encountered difficulty in maintaining consistent views of the prototype when these additional specifications were introduced.

We argue that the reason for these political tensions is that there is an interrelationship between the three dimensions of fidelity, audience, and development stage. Ignoring the significance of this relationship can lead to the kinds of tensions that we experienced when we tried to use a proto-type of a particular level of fidelity for different audiences, and at different stages of development. Whilst the prototype was suitable for us throughout the development process (so, fixed fidelity dimension, and fixed audience), we found that changing the audience dimension changed the requirements of the prototype. For example, the software development team required an additional level of detail not represented in the prototype. This change in audience was compounded by additionally changing the development phase e.g. using it to communicate with the technical team during testing.

Lesson 2: Different Audiences Require Different Representations

The way the wireframes were used in these projects was sufficient for communicating within the HCI team. To communicate with other stake-holders in the projects the representation needs to be targeted to effectively serve their aims.

Using wireframes when communicating with clients requires that the designers retain a focus on the issues concerning them. We have seen that clients may focus on domain specific details rather than the overall func-tionality and also that they may see this as the final design. To avoid the first problem it may be a good idea not to use the clients' products and domain language if possible. To avoid the latter it is important to make sure that the visual design is developed and discussed in parallel to the development of the wireframe. Thus, it may be better to use low-fidelity paper prototypes until the key navigational and content structure is agreed. (This in no way excludes input from users in helping to define that structure and content.)

On the contrary, when testing the wireframe with users one of the important factors is the domain language used on the site. If the users do not under-stand the language it will cause usability problems. Similarly, inconsistencies between the completeness of the visual design, navigation, functionality, and content can disorient users during testing. One solution would be to ensure that the prototypes are as close as possible to the final design. However, this would seem to defeat the point of iterative, incremental devel-opment. An alternative solution to this problem would be to use several representations in the initial usability testing, one for testing the flow (e.g. low-fidelity mock-ups), one for testing the brand (e.g. a graphical story-board), one for testing the domain language (e.g. a paper-prototype), and so on. However, it is also important to understand that it is not until the user can experience the combination of the three that any definitive conclusions can be made about the final user experience.

The wireframes were useful for communicating with software developers. However, they are not detailed enough to work on their own. In project B we used use cases as an additional means of communication and they proved to be very useful. However, using use cases without visual representations is not enough even for system developers since they give too much room for interpretations of the presentation and dynamics of the interaction. In Project A we annotated the wireframes for the technical development, and related these to the appropriate use cases. Thus, for software developers prototypes are best viewed as a core reference, supported by additional, more detailed, specifications.

References

Boehm BW (1988) "A Spiral Model of Software Development and Enhancement." IEEE Computer, 21(5):61–72

Hamilton F et al. (1998). Task-related principles for user interface design In: G. van der Veer (ed.) Proceedings of the Shaerding Workshop on Task Analysis, Austria, June 1998

Kruchten P (2000). The Rational Unified Process: An Introduction. Addison-Wesley-Longman, Inc, Reading, Massachusetts.

Newman MW and Landay JA (2000) Sitemaps, Storyboards, and Specifications: A Sketch of Web-site Design Practice. In Designing Interactive Systems, DIS 2000, New York City, August 2000 pp 263–274

PART 3

Politics and New Media: The Overwhelming Importance of Usability on the Web

The Politics of Intranet Usability: Can One Size Fit All?

10

Scott Gallacher, Robin Williams and Rob Procter

This case study follows the twists and turns in a corporate intranet application project within a large UK bank. It reveals decision-making – from the project's inception through to its development and testing – to be a highly politicized process as various players sought to use the project as a vehicle for pushing forward their own particular agendas. A key consequence of this was that usability issues – if they were considered at all at this time – often took second place to the needs of political deal making. That these deals were critical to gaining approval for the project seems undeniable, but they also jeopardized the prospects of achieving a usable application, often leaving usability staff to "pick up the pieces".

The case study illustrates the often highly political character of organizational IT projects, and demonstrates the importance for usability experts of getting involved at the earlier, formative stages of the project life cycle, when many of the decisions that will map out a project's organizational and technical trajectories are actually made. Though it is unlikely to challenge radically the political character of project decision-making processes, it would at least enable usability experts to become players. As other IT professionals have found out before them, to have responsibility without power is an unenviable position in which to find oneself in any organization (Fincham et al., 1994). Names have been changed throughout.

Introduction – "Do We Really Need an Intranet?"

Many studies have drawn attention to the threats to usability that frequently emerge in the design and development phases of IT projects (e.g. Poltrock and Grudin, 1994). This case study goes further by illustrating how, despite the rhetoric, usability issues continue to be treated as a side-show in many IT projects. It demonstrates how the capacity of project team members to satisfy usability requirements may be compromised by the often intensely political nature of processes that are instrumental in getting projects approved.

The immediate tactical aim of the project was to demonstrate the possibilities for delivering interactive, multimedia-based training materials to staff directly through the bank's branch network. The longer term, strategic aim of the project was rather more ambitious, being nothing less than to convince the bank's Executive Board that there was a sound business case for investing in the creation of a single, integrated corporate intranet. This was to have an important influence on the subsequent course of the project.

BigBank is a large UK bank that prides itself in having a strong track record in technical innovation. As our case study opens, BigBank's Technology Division had just successfully completed a pilot intranet project. Almost immediately, moves were afoot among certain players within Technology Division and the Bank's Corporate Communications department to get BigBank's board to approve the development of a full-scale, corporate intranet. While the pilot project had provided a useful, practical example of the benefits that an intranet could provide, the champions of the corporate intranet project would have to make a separate business case for this new investment. Building a business case for a corporate intranet would not be easy, as one of the project champions explained: "Justification for intranet systems is usually a soft case and this has to be sold to hard-nosed bankers. The cost-benefits of the system are often long term and difficult to quantify."

What the project champions needed was an application that would justify the investment by demonstrating real financial benefits. Having found it, they could then put together a coalition of political support and technical expertise that could ensure the project's survival and eventual success. In the process, they would have to make compromises over the project's technical specifications and set limits on its scope in order to deliver a usable and useful application.

Getting the Go Ahead: Cost, Timing and Glamour

The project champions found what they were looking for in the shape of a new, network-based training tool, the Network Training and Communications System (NTCS), with Corporate Communications as the project sponsor. In early lobbying for the project, its champions presented the following vision:

> Corporate Communications plans to revolutionise the Bank's training and communication strategy through an exciting business vision known as the Network Training and Communications Service (NTCS). In branches, NTCS will be delivered via one or more (depending on the size of the branch) PCs. These PCs will be powerful multimedia machines that run a web browser and have a "network" connection (yet to be fully defined). NTCS will support intranet access and interactive training and will provide the hardware, software and network framework for running and managing of (CD-based) multimedia training and collecting trainee data via the web browser. All these facilities will be accessed and managed via the web browser on the PC.

While this pitch evidently attempted to capitalize on the glamour of multimedia and the World Wide Web (WWW), in the event, what made NTCS so attractive to the bank's IT strategists was its timeliness. The expected imminent arrival of the Euro would soon necessitate widespread training for bank staff, an extremely costly investment as the Bank must pay not only for the instructors, but also for venues, and foot the transport and accommodation bill for trainees. In addition, the bank loses the work of that employee for the period of the course. Corporate Communications argued that delivering training over a corporate intranet, using NTCS, would greatly minimise or, in some cases, even eliminate these costs. One of the project champions explained the business case somewhat more prosaically as follows:

> The original benefits [of the earlier pilot intranet project] were the cost of printing the phone book, calls to switchboard, directory enquiries calls. With the combination of training, costs were saved regarding costs of transport and accommodation incurred sending people for training plus the time lost through them being away.

Mobilizing Support and Getting Approval

With the broad business aims established and a project sponsor in place, it was still necessary to carry out a feasibility study of the solution proposed. This would in itself require a budget, but with the desired level of interest achieved this was now easily found. The aim of the study was to cost out the project and investigate technical, usability and logistic issues. Regarding the latter, within an organization as large as BigBank, it was important that communication was organised and actions co-ordinated between relevant organizational players. As one of the project champions explained:

> There are three components to any project within the Bank: the business and the Technology Division, which has two sections – System Development and IT Services. System Development people manage the relationship, getting the requirements and designing the system, while IT Services handle the infrastructure for that technology. In this project there has been a very open dialogue between these sections.

Meetings were arranged with members of these key organizational players and a network created within the bank that would support the project. A major selling point to them was the opportunity to be involved in a potentially high profile project that would advance their individual positions. By securing this involvement, the project champions sought to circumvent anyone raising problematic issues at a later stage and arguing against the project. This "buy-in" would be crucial to the project gaining final approval.

The inclusion of usability investigations at this formative stage of the project was a promising sign that usability issues would receive the attention they deserve. However, even here, political considerations held sway. The results of these investigations were used selectively such that those which demonstrated the project in a positive light were put to the fore, whereas those that raised questions, or showed up problems in the project in some way were set to one side. Only lip service was paid to the practical lessons learnt, with guidelines traded off against political needs.

PC or TV? – The Vision Is Compromised

In order to clinch the all-important blessing of the BigBank board to progress from the feasibility study to the project proper, however, the project champions found themselves having to retreat on some of the original plans which left the project having to grapple with significant technical legacy issues.

First, because of the fundamental importance of the content for the application (in this case the training materials), it was important to use a medium that would allow uncomplicated migration from the previous method of delivery to the new one. Trainers up, until that point, had worked in a classroom environment operating lecture style delivery with slides in Powerpoint format. It was possible to use this medium directly within the new system, but it was not the most effective format. HTML pages were preferred as they allowed a greater degree of flexibility and placed less load on the bank's network. As a result of discussions with the lead trainer, it was decided that opting for the Powerpoint medium would be the most pragmatic option at that point. It was reasoned that because the new system was providing a large "culture shock" for the present trainers, it was important to ease their entry into the new system as much as possible. The use of the already familiar Powerpoint system would allow this as well as eliminating a need for immediate retraining of the trainers that would add to the forecast cost. This compromise would also, critically, provide the system with immediately suitable material and assure the support of the trainers.

Second, and perhaps most crucially, the project champions had to agree to dilute the intranet delivery concept. Originally, the NTCS project team had planned to use Microsoft's Netshow to create and deliver the audio-video broadcast content over the intranet, which would allow the whole system to be delivered through a single point of access: the desktop PC, as well as allowing for future technical advances. The feasibility study had demonstrated that this would be possible. However, the sizeable prior investment in the Bank's own TV network (BigBankTV) made this financially and politically inexpedient.

To pursue the original plan would "tread on the toes" of BigBank TV, as one of the project leaders put it. BigBankTV used a very expensive, leased satellite link to broadcast to TV sets in each branch from a central studio run by Corporate Affairs. The project had been very costly (in the region of £3,000,000) and was widely regarded in the bank as an "ego trip" on the part of the Board since it was widely seen as providing only a short-term technical solution. Corporate Affairs realized, however, that if they integrated the new system with BigBankTV it would appeal to the Board, by making the new system appear more cost effective, and thereby also strengthening its political support. In the event, it was decided to incorporate BigBankTV into NTCS, using the BigBankTV network to broadcast training classes into the branches. One of the project team explained:

"When we first looked at NTCS, we looked at NetShow Theatre as well as NetMeeting. We came back to the business and said 'if you want it in its current state . . . then it will probably cost an extra £100,000 with servers and management etc.' The business said 'No, we would rather maximize our investment in satellite TV.' Undoubtedly at some point in the future we'll look at putting it all on the network as satellite time is so expensive."

As with the decision to use Powerpoint, this created restrictions for NTCS that would compromise its usability. This solution required the incorporation of the TV into the intranet set up, requiring trainees to monitor two displays simultaneously. It allowed little scope for future development. While NTCS was made technically weaker and less usable by this change, the case for it was conversely made much stronger and, in the end, it was this consideration that carried the day.

Political Trade-Offs: More Expertise Means Less Control

With the project approved and budgets in place, the next important task for the NTCS project team was to gather the resources to undertake the work. The biggest problem that the team was faced with was gathering the skill base it would need to implement the project. This would require delicate manoeuvring on the part of the project leaders as they sought to balance the political need to harness the support of various in-house players against the sometimes superior expertise and experience available through external suppliers.

The bank's Technology Division wasn't best equipped to provide the multimedia/web technology skills needed for the project, as this was still relatively virgin territory for them. As a project team member was to comment later: "We're gradually skilling up. These skills are in such demand. There's always the temptation to go to third party providers but I feel morally we have to keep as much of the work in-house because if we don't start skilling up our people in these technologies we're going to be in trouble"

The alternative was to buy in the expertise needed from outside. During the feasibility study stage of the project, interested parties in BT had heard of the planned project. The consultancy wing of BT decided it was a project that they should tender for. Bypassing the usual channels, they approached Corporate Communications directly to arrange a meeting. Corporate Communications agreed, underlining its position of strength by reminding the Technology Division that it wasn't the "only game in town" and would have to tender like everyone else. News of this development created fears within the project inner circle (essentially the feasibility team) that they would find themselves ceding control to BT, and with it much of the share of the credit they hoped would accrue from a successful project. With a heightened sense of urgency, they set about the task of eliminating the threat posed by BT by putting together a rival array of expertise. At the same time, the NTCS team used its inside knowledge of the project to press on with its development in order to make it more time consuming to bring in a third party who would need to retrace the progress made.

Since it would take the Technology Division time to assemble the necessary skills and experience, the only solution would be to recruit an alternative, external party, one that could be controlled more easily than the likes of BT. Having (perhaps unwittingly) motivated the search for an alternative external partner, Corporate Communications now came up with the solution. JNM is a small software house based in the south of England. Its principal product was a presentation system that had the capability to register and poll responses and provide an immediate graphical representation of the results. This system had been widely used at various conferences throughout the UK and JNM was reputedly the leader in this field. It was via its conference work that it had come into contact with representatives from Corporate Communications who were taken by the slick graphical representations and interactivity. When they decided to pursue intranet-based training, they decided that this was a feature well worth incorporating.

A closer examination of JNM's system revealed several shortcomings for the NTCS project, however. Developed for use in an isolated conference scenario, it had very limited capacity in its current form to be re-scaled for use within a large organization. In the circumstances, however, the project feasibility team agreed that using JNM would prove beneficial for the image of the project and politically, even though acknowledging among themselves that NTCS would be more successfully developed in-house without JNM's involvement. Technical considerations had to be balanced against the political situation and Corporate Communications was keen to involve JNM. The involvement of JNM would undoubtedly provide benefits in selling the project as it could present a system that already existed and which could be demonstrated, and this would understandably carry more weight than assurances that a new system could be built.

Two more pieces of the expertise jigsaw remained to be put in place. The importance of content within the NTCS meant that the involvement of the Training Unit was vital. As the project gained approval, the Training Unit was consulted to provide a more direct input into the system. It was also important to allay their fears on the effect that it would have on their jobs. The project leader commented: "At first they were a bit frightened and didn't understand (the system). You're taking people who have spent 20 years of their working lives teaching people in classrooms, then throwing all this technology at them and saying – 'this is how we want you to do it now'."

In order to enlist the full support of the Training Unit, the NTCS team sought to involve them in the decision-making and design process, but also needed to moderate this process. To this end they created close working ties with one of the senior trainers, who acted as the chief point of contact and managed communication between the two sections. The project leader again: "Some of them were a bit scared at first but we had the senior trainer . . . She would get suggestions from the other trainers then discuss them with us. Then she would go back, let them know what was feasible and the possibilities and so on. It worked very well."

In another politically motivated decision, trainers were the only end user group consulted at this time. Those who would use the system in the role of trainees were excluded from involvement in determining the system requirements. This was because while the trainers' support was vital to the project's survival, that of end users was not, and the project leadership was fearful that if trainees were involved at this stage, conflicting requirements might emerge and derail the project.

The final expertise required was that of user interface design. The Learning Technologies Department (LTD) had been created as an arm of the Bank's Human Resources department, and specialized in the production of multi-media CDs to be distributed for use by stand-alone clients in the branches. This was an area in which the Technology Division had no capability or skills and so LTD had been allowed to grow autonomously. With the initiation of the NTCS project, however, as multimedia technology moved towards networked systems incorporating web technologies capable of interactive training, it was inevitable that the interests of LTD and the Technology Division would overlap and eventually conflict. In the circumstances, it was not difficult to convince LTD, who had felt very threatened by the project, to take on the job of user interface design. As the project leader explained: "We said – 'look, we're just technologists, we can make it work and you just design the screens. Tell us what you want it to look like, paint the picture and we can do it'. We backed off doing any 'look and feel', we're not experts in that."

The chief technical expert of LTD actually carried out the work. It is only at this point that we find that a usability expert finally gets involved. The project leader noted how: "Jim Smith did the screen design based on what the senior trainer (who was representing a whole bunch of trainers) had advised. Jim has a good eye for usability anyway – that's his key skill."

Just when it seemed that the project was heading for a successful conclusion, however, the consequences of some of the earlier compromises finally became apparent as the project moved into the testing and role out phases.

Testing and Roll Out: "Keep It Simple" Wins the Day

The decision to use BigBankTV required that TVs and PCs be located within the branches in mutually accessible places, and this was eventually to prove a considerable stumbling block. The original placement of the TVs within the Branches had been chosen to allow the whole of the staff to view BigBankTV broadcasts, whereas meeting the needs of an interactive training system required a more isolated setting. The Bank's Property department established that moving the TV with fittings and connections to a location that was compatible with both purposes would be very costly, and even physically impossible in some branches. So, late in the day, the NTCS team returned to the aim of incorporating the TV image within the PC. A number of ways of achieving this were identified:

- TV tuner card to feed the signal into the PC for display on the screen.

- A system for delivering images via networks using new technology that was unproven, but was backed by BT.

- A second system for delivering images via networks using technology that was proven, but from a supplier unknown in the UK.

In the event, both the network-based suggestions were rejected because, in their different ways, they were judged to be too risky at this late stage in the project lifecycle. This left the first option of using the TV tuner card, which was not as forward looking as the other options, but was proven and did not require direct integration with the system.

The project survived this final alarm, and was eventually successfully rolled out into the branches. However, it is clear that this outcome owed little to a systematic, principled and early consideration of usability issues and rather more to the project team's capacity to salvage something from a crisis. Though this particular project was considered a success, we argue that coping with usability threats as they arise is, in general, a risky strategy for usability staff to pursue. Instead, they need to become more politically aware and seek out organizational positions that will enable them to foreground usability issues from the very beginning.

Lessons Learned

- Many of the decisions that will map out a project's organizational and technical trajectories are actually made as the key players struggle to get the project approved.

- These decision-making processes are often shaped by the immediate exigencies of organizational (and inter-organizational) politics, with the result that usability issues can easily be subordinated to other concerns.

- The implications for usability of decisions made at these early stages in a project can be hard to undo.

- To counter these problems, usability experts should be prepared to get involved at these formative stages of the project life cycle.

- This is unlikely to challenge the political character of project decision-making processes, but it would at least enable usability experts to become players and so acquire some power to match their responsibilities.

References

Fincham R, Fleck J, Procter R, Scarbrough H, Tierney M and Williams R (1994). Expertise and Innovation: IT Strategies in the Financial Services Sector. Oxford University Press, New York

Poltrock S and Grudin J (1994). Organizational Obstacles to Interface Design and Development. ACM Transactions on Computer-Human Interaction, 1(1):52–60

Developing Intranets Which People Use: Making Progress when Everyone Has an Opinion

Lucy Suits and Lee Zukor

The goal of an intranet site is to improve knowledge sharing and productivity. In a large company, it can be difficult to achieve consensus on how to make this happen. Knowledge management experts, information systems project managers, graphic designers, marketing leaders, HTML developers and usability engineers are used to fighting for their places, convinced that they know best. In truth, the intranet is not yet mature, and there are no definite answers. This chapter describes experiences with the intranet sites of two Fortune 500 companies. In both cases, the usability engineer was a consultant from outside the company, in one case part of a team of consultants and in the other working more closely with company employees. Both intranet projects were riddled with mishaps, bad decisions, personality conflicts, and compromises. Still, the usability engineers were able to improve the sites by becoming members of the project teams, and by tirelessly incorporating usability in everything they did.

Introduction: the Case Studies

A short description of each of our case studies helps keep them separate. Throughout the chapter, we refer to them as Example A and Example B.

Example A

In Example A, the usability engineers were employees who were acting as consultants to a larger project team made up of company employees. The usability engineers were brought onto the project specifically to give usability feedback and design input. Most decision-making power in this situation was held by high-level company executives. Unrealistic expectations and access to users were considerable challenges to this project.

Example B

In Example B, the usability engineers were members of an external consulting team tasked with providing the client with a complete intranet solution. Turnover at the client site and changing expectations were major hurdles to completing this work.

Throughout the chapter we will compare the consultants' experiences in the following areas:

- Setting expectations.
- Identifying and accessing users.
- Defining roles within the project.
- Balancing opinion with evidence.
- Being flexible.
- Building the "right" Project Team.

Our experience suggests that the most successful usability engineers are those who:

- Create realistic expectations.
- Apply best practices.
- Think creatively.
- Enjoy their work but do not take feedback personally.
- Understand that usability is only one factor in a successful site.
- Leave their egos at the door.
- Speak plainly, rather than in "usability speak".
- Know when to compromise and when to say no.

Setting Expectations

In large companies, intranet projects are politically charged. It is imperative that the Usability Team creates clear expectations from the outset of the project: goals for the site, type of information needed, information gathering methods, usability deliverables, number of resources, time/cost commitment, and timeframe. Setting expectations includes being clear about what the team will not deliver.

In Example A, high level executives (CEO (Chief Executive Officer), president, and CIO (Chief Information Officer) created the expectations for the intranet. As a result, before the design team was built, key design and usability goals had already been established. This included:

- Colour schemes determined by marketing branding requirements (company colours, for example).
- A high-level navigation structure to match a picture the CEO had seen in a book about knowledge management.
- Project schedules established by the CEO, who wanted to "see what we can put together in 60 days".

Although navigation, schedules and colour choices had been established, other key information was noticeably missing. For example:

Why Did We Need a Knowledge Repository?

Everyone was eager to create a robust intranet, but no one had a clear idea of why. In fact, we couldn't even agree on what knowledge management was, or what information was suitable for the web.

Who Was Our User Base?

How could we hone in on our users, rather than trying to design for "anybody who wants to use the site"? We needed to understand their environment, their skills and their needs.

What Can Our Systems Do?

We needed to have a clear understanding of what technologies were available to us and to our users.

The first thing that our usability engineers did was to create expectations of their own. These expectations included what deliverables they would be providing and how long each would take to create. The so-called "User Centred Design Team" included two to three graphic designers and two to three content editors. We quickly decided to put two Usability Engineers on the project: one took the lead on information design issues and the other led usability testing. Keeping the group small made it easy to shift focus as was (frequently) necessary.

The next piece of business related to project timing. The project schedule itself, imposed from above, was not negotiable. It was up to us to decide how much time it would take to make the intranet site usable. Being full-time members of the project team made it easier for us to get the information we needed. It also helped us to earn the trust of the other team members, and to take on support roles that were, at times, outside our usual responsibilities. In addition, given the rapid delivery schedule, we determined that immediate, regular feedback would be most useful to the team. As a result, we conducted many quick studies rather than one or two formal tests.

Unfortunately, other issues were not so easily resolved. The terms "UCD" and "Usability" were often used interchangeably. As part of the larger design team of writers and visual designers, it was difficult to establish who did what on a project and make clear the difference between a "fresh set of eyes" and a usability expert. Project leaders were confused and graphic designers and content editors met the team's usability inquiries with blank stares. Since the burden of creating a shared language fell squarely on our shoulders, the usability engineers learned and used "developer-speak" – to be understood, and to be taken seriously. That said, as a result, it was never clear whether the intranet project team had a clear understanding of usability concepts.

Example B is made up of two independent project teams working together to complete a site. In this case, working relationships were aggravated when the people who signed off on the project left the company before work had begun in earnest. If unclear expectations were a challenge in our first example, they were even more so here. The project manager who originally signed the contract for the intranet site left the client's company, and was replaced by a new project manager with her own views and expectations.

The project kick-off and requirements gathering meeting was derailed when the new project manager announced that the requirements gathering phase was complete and directed the usability engineer to begin designing immediately. With a 6-week timeline and a dwindling budget, it was difficult to convince the client otherwise. The resulting intranet site was built around the company's organization chart rather than by how its customers needed to access information. End-users were left out of the process entirely.

Usability engineers need access to specific information about users and requirements. In both of our examples, this access was denied.

In Example A, the project leadership was more interested in learning intranet best practices than in finding out about its own user base. But when were best practices applicable and when did we need to do actual field research? In the retail industry, many users work in warehouses, stock rooms, and stores. It was important to incorporate these factors into the intranet design. Our teams would have done well to observe users surreptitiously, which would have been easy to accomplish in stores.

In Example B, the project deadline drove the entire process. Questions about requirements were perceived as wasting time that could have been spent in development. But we could have gathered customer information by asking our questions in different ways, as described in the next section.

What we learned is this: as usability professionals, we need to remain focused on both of our customers – those who support our project involvement (project managers) and those who will ultimately determine the success or failure of the product itself (users). Our challenge is often to find a way to meet the needs of both groups. We can do this by setting appropriate expectations – and by finding creative ways to gather the information we need.

Identifying and Getting Access to Users

Successful intranet projects require access to users. In situations where this is discouraged, information may have to be gathered covertly. In situations where this is strictly forbidden, it is important to understand the limits and to find creative ways to work within them.

Identifying users of an intranet is as difficult as it is crucial. Getting access to them is more so. This proved to be a real challenge in Example A for several reasons. As is often the case, the project owners were concerned that employees would come to expect too much of the new portal. As a result, the usability engineers were told not to show associates prototypes or concepts that might "get their hopes up." Attempts at gathering information through field studies were repeatedly denied. The usability engineers were not to create any expectations at all, but to generate excitement whenever possible.

What to do? The project leaders repeatedly described themselves and the developers as typical users, suggesting that the team observe them instead of going out to the stores. The usability engineers accepted the offer and treated the observations as sales opportunities. In one example, the usability engineers observed a project leader retrieving information from the newly designed intranet site. After conducting the observation, the usability engineers described the type of information that could be provided by actual (rather than representative) users, and how a fresh set of eyes might be useful. Eventually, the project leaders referred the usability engineers to customers who could be relied on to provide less biased feedback.

We took every possible opportunity to educate the business and technology sides of the project on the types of information that we could gather through field studies. One of the most difficult concepts for us to land was that users could provide us with useful information about their use of the intranet even if they had never used it. For example, users could have let us observe their current work areas, showing us their offices, allowing us to understand what systems they used and how an intranet site could make their lives easier. These educational opportunities challenged our ability to remain positive and resilient. At times we spent more time complaining about our limited role than working to make the best of it. We should have visited the retail environment and gathered the information we needed any way we could.

In Example B, the usability engineer had access to the current site's webmaster and the supervisor of the employees who were most likely to use the site. Both of these people were invaluable resources. Although the client's Project Manager had forbidden the usability engineer from asking these experts what the site would be used for, the usability engineer was able to gather this information by asking good, carefully framed questions about the underlying technology. The usability engineer initially asked what type of files were being accessed on the site and then followed up with a questions about how the users would use the files and what the users' needs were for the files. The subject matter experts didn't share the project managers' ideas that all the analysis was already complete and were therefore willing to discuss the users' need with the usability engineer. This data, covertly gathered and analysed, was used to build a solid information architecture, which was critical to the success of the site.

Defining Roles Within the Project

Intranet project roles should be clearly defined at the outset of the project. This includes an understanding of job titles and of what each person adds to the project mix. It also includes an understanding of overlapping skills, and boundaries around their expectations of each other.

In Example A, two-thirds of the User-Centred Design group consisted of content writers and artists who were not familiar with the term UCD. The usability engineers were challenged to find their place within the group, to help clarify the difference between roles on the team, and to incorporate usability engineering techniques wherever possible.

To successfully integrate themselves with the rest of the team, the usability engineers worked to understand the value that each team member provided. Each person's role was considered equally valuable and respected, and each team member was encouraged to think outside of his or her role, even if his or her opinions were sometimes overruled. Focusing on the common goal helped promote a combined sense of ownership and teamwork that has extended throughout many different projects to this day. Still, the usability engineers should have gone one step further. Clarifying the role of each team member *in writing* would have formalized the plan, defining it clearly from the outset. For example:

> *Usability Engineer:* Conducts field studies and other observations, creates conceptual models, researches best practices, conducts heuristic evaluations of early design models and concepts, content (text, links, etc.), and navigation, provides the team with design feedback throughout the project.

> *Visual Designer:* Creates intranet graphics, selects colours, fonts, and other graphical elements (buttons, links, etc.).

> *Content Provider:* Writes all of the text that appears on the site, including text blocks, link names, button names, and banners, if included.

It is less important that the information be well written than that it be clear. In Example A, the usability engineers found that true working definitions were more appropriate than those you might find in a textbook. If the members of the project team feel that there is overlap in roles, for example, writing these issues down is a good way to ensure that they are dealt with. Doing so at the start of a project helps establish working relationships, expectations, and limits. A "roles" document can also help the project leader to understand who is responsible for what tasks.

People's familiarity with these roles is another critical factor. In our Example B, none of the consulting company's project team had worked together before. Although the roles of Project Manager, Technical Manager, and Developer were well established within the consulting company, all of the people filling these roles were new employees. To make matters worse, the concepts of usability engineering and information architecture were new to the consulting company as well, so no one quite knew how to integrate them into the process. The lack of clarity regarding roles within the consulting company was amplified when external clients became involved.

After the usability engineer created several page layouts, the visual designer created three concepts for the client to review. One of these concepts deviated drastically from the layouts – the navigation was on the right side of the screen. Although the usability engineer had made it clear to the visual designer that the right side navigation was not usable, she was on vacation when the concepts were presented. The client loved the uniqueness of the right side navigation model and selected it as the framework for the site. If the visual designer trusted the usability engineer and clearly understood the implications of an unusuable design, he might never have recommended the unorthodox design to the customer.

In addition, the usability engineer should have provided the team with extensive data supporting her page layouts. The team could have referred to this when the usability engineer was out of town.

Combating Opinion with Evidence

Many intranets are built because "everyone else is doing it" or because an executive saw its potential at a conference or in an article. The fact is that we do design for vice-presidents, and acknowledging this can help to eliminate some professional frustration.

Internally-focused sites cause companies to end up with home pages full of mission statements, photos of the CEO, and corporate history (all of which do fit on an "about this company" page; just not on the home page). No company is the centre of the universe for its customers, and to focus excessively on internal matters ignores the reality of the business world. Even so, single individuals do have the power to make decisions based entirely on their own perceptions. In Example A, the intranet was built specifically because an executive saw it that way at a conference. In Example B, the intranet was built because an executive decided the old intranet needed a fresh look and additional information. Accepting these realities might have saved our groups a lot of heartache.

The fact that high level executives were making important intranet decisions meant that things the team might have taken for granted sometimes required an enormous amount of supporting research. In Example A, to convince the team that flashing banners were inappropriate, the usability engineers presented the project leaders with articles regarding best practices and data from usability studies. The usability engineers used the same technique to justify font sizes and colours. Each small battle was viewed as an opportunity to educate the company. When presented with compelling evidence, even the most self-assured executives can be swayed.

In Example A, the usability engineers educated company executives by gathering information about best practices, conducting "stealth" usability evaluations, and giving presentations whenever possible. Eventually, the executives began to understand the reasons behind the team's designs, and to understand that their decisions were not necessarily correct, even if they were final. Educated executives quickly became the company's greatest usability proponents, spreading the word powerfully. The usability engineers' small investment of time and research went a long way towards solidifying their position in the company.

In Example B, the only contact that the usability engineer had with the company's executives was at the kick-off meeting. She chose to educate the project team, hoping that the information would trickle up, and it did. Using the same techniques of persistence, presentations, and solid data, the usability engineer convinced the project team of the power of usability evaluations. In her next project with the same client, usability tests were a required part of the project plan.

In both examples, executives maintained strict ownership of the sites and the right to approve or disapprove of all designs. Still, by viewing each setback as an opportunity, usability engineers were able to improve their sites considerably.

Being Flexible

When given the choice between creating a perfect product that is never released and an imperfect project that benefits its customers, we must consistently choose the latter. There is a point at which our insistence on a complete usability process becomes counterproductive. The most successful usability engineers can quickly assess a situation and impose the parts of the process that make the most sense, given project constraints.

In Example A, the usability engineers were alarmed and discouraged by the direction the project was heading. The UCD team was inexperienced, and its visual designers and writers had all worked together on a previous product that was poorly designed and not well accepted by users. Access to users was severely limited, and there was no time to conduct formal usability studies. The usability engineers worried that their data was not good enough and that the users were not involved enough. They spent the first two weeks fighting with the project team and the next two weeks fighting the requirements. By the time the usability engineers were through fighting, their schedule had slipped by nearly four weeks. In Example B, the entire project timeline was six weeks. There was no time to fight, only to adapt. The challenge was figuring out how to provide value despite unchanging, imposed guidelines.

In both examples, usability engineers realized that they could offer significant help in several areas. They did this by:

- Clearly understanding the project goals, including scheduling constraints, user constraints, and project ownership.

- Quickly establishing what work they could provide within the project constraints. If the usability engineers could not conduct full-blown designs sessions and usability tests, what elements of those things could they incorporate into their work? They chose to provide a series of quick heuristic evaluations, to research best practices for similar projects, to post questions to a usability listserv, to interview users under the guise of another project, and to interview subject matter experts when no users were available.

- Being flexible enough to understand and work within the project constraints. Usability engineers researched best practices and provided immediate feedback whenever possible.

- Resisting the temptation to suffer through meetings silently, consistently voicing concerns, gently but persistently reminding the rest of the team of their roles and skills.

Understanding that neither project would support the rigor of true user-centred design work, the usability engineers continued to guide team meetings in a more user-centred direction, representing users and incorporating usability concepts and techniques whenever possible. The usability engineers became extremely flexible in their schedules and work styles. In both examples, flexibility and customer focus yielded positive results. By working within the confines of their projects, the usability engineers were perceived as valuable team members, rather than as impractical or uncooperative team players.

Building the "Right" Project Team

The best usability engineer for a project is one who is intelligent and flexible, and one who is not controlled by ego. The usability engineer should have excellent negotiation skills, and should be able to present a compelling case for the work.

The right project team includes members with a variety of roles and hard and soft skills. Equally important, the right project team includes at least one firm supporter of usability. This person should be in a leadership position, and should be firmly convinced of the benefits of usability engineering.

In Example A, the usability engineers never became fully integrated with the project team. There were several reasons for this. First, the management team did not include a firm supporter of usability. Although they included usability in the project plan, they did not implement or support making changes to the system or the project schedule based on usability issues. In addition, the usability engineers on the project tended to be timid, and often approached their work complaining about what they could not do, instead of working to figure out how they could provide value to the project. The right project team in this case would have been one with stronger management support and more persistent, positive-thinking usability engineers.

In Example B, the intranet project team was a combination of two independent, already established teams: the consultants and the clients. The majority of the consulting group was made up of new consultants, many of whom did not have a clear understanding of how to integrate the usability engineer role within their own team. The clients had very few people to dedicate to the project, and had no flexibility with resources if the team failed to gel.

Still, what made this the "right" project team was the consistent, open sharing of information. Despite its shortcomings, the project team worked well together by educating, communicating, and negotiating. Team members listened to each other and shared what they knew about the project. Open communication led to trust within the team. As mis-communications, mis-perceptions and other mistakes occurred, the team talked through them, working towards resolutions without egos getting in the way. This assured the highest level of success on the project, and created a basis for ongoing understanding.

In our next projects for the company in Example A, we have had enormous success by allowing project leaders to interview potential usability engineering candidates. This gives the project leaders a strong sense of resource ownership, and eliminates the resentment they can feel when resources are imposed on their projects without their approval. An initial interview ensures immediate buy-in, and in these situations, the usability engineer starts out as a more integral and integrated team member, laying the groundwork for success.

Summary

Both teams were riddled with mishaps, bad decisions, personality conflicts, and compromises. But all of these things translated into learning opportunities. We learned that, rather than demand access to users, we could be creative about how to get good feedback from them. We learned to create realistic expectations from the outset of our projects and then to be flexible. We learned that working with the "right" project team is something to strive for, but that, in reality, there are no perfect teams. In reality, a positive attitude and open communication will move the team forward, even when circumstances make this difficult. Intranet projects require usability engineers to leave their egos behind, think creatively, and understand when to compromise and when to stand firm. Intranet work provides unique challenges, but also provides many exciting opportunities.

Lessons Learned

In our intranet experience, the most successful usability engineers:

- Become members of the project teams rather than outside observers. This means that, although they incorporated usability in everything they did, Usability Engineers had a broad understanding of the project and contributed wherever there was a need.

- Create realistic expectations for the projects and project teams that they are on. This can include goals for the site, the type of information needed, information gathering methods, usability deliverables, and timeframe.

- Think creatively in order to provide the project team with flexible solutions and regular feedback. Successful usability engineers view challenges as opportunities, and spend little time complaining about the project and the team.

- Enjoy creating quality work, but continually look at their designs from other perspectives and are open to constructive feedback. Intranet projects are politically charged by nature, and always involve extensive give and take.

- Understand both of their customers – those who support our project involvement (project managers) and those who will ultimately determine the success or failure of the product itself (users) – and look for ways to meet their needs.

- See themselves as educators, and work at spreading the gospel of usability day after day.

Getting Past the Home Page: Structuring Information with People in Mind

12

Karen Gunter

Identifying the major defects of a web-site is comparatively easy. The difficult part of web-site usability improvement is managing the organizational politics involved in implementing change. This chapter describes the Rural-Net project, part of a European Union (EU) funded initiative which focused on the use of web technologies in rural areas to improve the social and economic well-being of local residents and businesses. It illustrates the difficulties of trying to please many stakeholders, and discusses the importance of structuring information in a way which speaks the users' language, a vital component for easy navigation of a web-site, especially for inexperienced users. No real names are used throughout.

Introduction: The Web and the Rise of Usability

The profile of usability work in the IT industry is higher now than it has ever been. Where once in-house HCI (human computer interaction) specialists were only a feature of certain blue chip hardware and software companies, "customer experience teams" can now be found throughout the e-business sector. In-house usability consultants were at one time a rarity, compared to external consultants, but are now increasingly common. Demand for usability professionals has never been higher and discussion of usability issues is commonplace. On this evidence readers would be forgiven for assuming that the battle for usable web-sites had been won and that user needs are given priority in the e-business sector. In reality the practice of usability has far to go and is still largely dictated by the politics of its environment.

So why this increased interest in usability in the context of the web? It can be assigned to the growth of the online population – 49 per cent of all British adults now have access to the Internet either at home or work, an increase from 29 per cent just 2 years ago (Guardian ICM Survey January 2000). The Internet as the medium and web-sites as the message have expanded well beyond the "techie" users they were originally designed for, to become a truly mass medium with significant commercial and technological potential. However, that potential will not be realized if target audiences cannot use the technology easily.

This chapter uses a case study, fictitiously known as Rural Net, to discuss some of the common problems encountered in web-site usability improvement and consultancy. It should be emphasized that although some of the issues are unique to this project, the generality of its problems are not. Neither were the people involved on the project any better or worse than usual.

The Politics of Rural Net : One Web-Site, Many Owners

Rural Net is a pan-European project (partly funded by the European Union) which involved participants from rural regions in four countries. Web-sites were produced for each of the four regions and although not identical, the original aim was that they should share some commonality in approach, delivery and use of technology. With the passage of time and the imperative of local needs this requirement gradually became less significant.

The focus on the use of web technologies in rural areas was to improve the social and economic well being of local residents and businesses. The principal application areas were:

● support for small and medium sized business;

● local and public services;

● lifelong learning;

● community networking and information.

The idea was that the Rural Net web-site should give the local community seamless access to various types of information offered by regional content providers, who in this case consisted of the local council, the Enterprise Board, the tourist board and police force. The aim of the content providers was to use the Web to provide a better service to the public.

Each region was committed to installing a number of regional access terminals to allow the public to use the site, for example, libraries, tourist information and enterprise board offices. This decision ensured that a high percentage of people accessing the site would be naïve users, whose experience of using web technology was limited.

Rural Net had a range of parties involved in its production:

● A technical lead, a small software house responsible for day-to-day development of the site.

● The regional content providers, who were also in essence the clients.

● Industrial sponsors, two large IT services companies who provided practical consultancy as their contribution to the project.

The author's involvement with Rural Net came about as part of this industrial sponsorship. In addition to usability consultancy, the industrial sponsors provided project management and development skills. There were a number of key themes that were considered important in the planning of the web-site, these were:

● *The integration of information,* both at a technical level ("integrate these two databases") and an organizational level ("get these two organizations to work together for the good of the local area").

● *Personalization:* users could register on the site. Registered members would have the ability to request specific types of news, to save search results and to bookmark links. It was anticipated that this feature would be particularly useful at the regional access points where a number of different users would use the same machine.

● *The use of a map style interface* to present geographical information to the user.

The nature of the project and its funding meant that there was a wide range of people involved, whose interests and goals did not always match. The technical lead (a small software company) and a research group at a local university were both reliant on funding from the project. They regarded it primarily as a research opportunity. The content providers wanted a site that supported the local community and local businesses, they were keen to have a practical easy to use site which would have a life beyond EU funding.

Structuring Information: Content Labels which Speak the Users' Language

The project partners met at a special interest group where they could discuss progress and contribute their ideas for the Rural Net site. Many of the partners were new to the web and did not have a strong idea of what they could expect from the technology; they had even less experience of what their end users would find acceptable. This scenario is fairly common in the current development of commercial web-sites, and unless checked can open the way to some serious usability problems.

It is important that information on a web-site is structured appropriately and in a way that a wide range of users will understand. Oblique content labels and cul de sacs are still a big problem with many web-sites: search and use of content labels are the two main ways in which users navigate a web-site (Rosenfeld and Morville, 1998). Users' (especially naïve users') browsing and searching strategies are still very much based on the analogy of printed media.

An unambiguous information architecture is the key to the usability of a Web-site. Information architecture is a topic which is much discussed in industry at the moment but in many cases it is not practised effectively. This could be due to the fact that good information architects are hard to find. The qualities required include a good technical understanding of the structuring of information plus an ability to see things from the users' perspective. (Many usability consultants fulfil a dual role including that of information architect.)

Early Problems: Whose Mental Model Is It, Anyway?

In the case of Rural Net problems arose early on with the development of the original interface to the web-site. This was based on user actions, with a button bar whose topic heading represented verbs rather than nouns.

Consequently, the interface was centred around a number of actions – *enquire, submit, pay, notify* and *monitor.* These actions could have a number of interpretations that were entirely subjective and dependent on the users' interpretation of the actions that they wished to perform. For instance: in the case of a user checking their local Council tax bill, would this be an enquiry, monitoring a payment, submitting a payment or paying? It assumed a particular mental model for users which was in practice impossible to predict. This problem was further exacerbated by the fact that none of the content providers were in a position to provide the specific functions promised by the action style topic headings.

The content providers were not happy with the original action-based interface. They anticipated that their end users would be put off by the use of language such as: "Citizen's View" and "Technical Annex". Structuring the site in this way also made the assumption that people would not visit Rural Net out of idle curiosity but with a clear goal of what they wished to achieve.

The original interface also included a personalization process, which gave the impression that new users must go through a registration procedure to access the site. Given that the site was sponsored by local government and the police, asking visitors for personal details could be seen as intrusive, although in fact, registration was optional and the intention was to help people viewing the site from public access terminals to save their favourite options.

The site also included a map style interface which gave access to geographical information in the region. This application had to be downloaded – a slow and tedious process which most users would give up on. The application itself was idiosyncratic and difficult to use.

Finally, there was no adequate help or site map and the search facility did not work. Given the obliqueness of the site's content headings this made Rural Net extremely difficult for the average user to navigate.

Project Management Means Managing Conflicts of Interest

Many of the project's problems occurred through the bureaucratic way in which it had been set up. European union funding procedures and the plans required to get and maintain EU funding are based around supporting a large bureaucracy rather than supporting effective project management. Rural Net was not unique in this, new technology projects do not fit well with old style management procedures.

EU guidelines set specific targets for outputs, but the project lacked any coherent project management plan or practical imperatives on the usability and design of the site. A good example of this was usability testing: the EU plan specified that this should be carried out (by a local university), however it was scheduled in near the end of the project, when there would be very little scope or commitment to change the existing web-site. There was no understanding that usability activities need to be co-ordinated with development activities in order to achieve product improvement. Similarly, day-to-day project management was not well coordinated. The overall effect was that the project was heavy on bureaucracy but low on efficiency.

Effective, supportive and professional project management is a vital component in the success of any well run software project. When that project incorporates elements of user centred design and usability, project management skills become even more vital.

Web-site development projects require a particular blend of project management skills to enable usability considerations to be accommodated. The project manager must have an understanding of the scope and importance of usability work and know the right points at which to apply usability consultancy. Most importantly they must have the "soft" interpersonal skills to convince the client of the need for the usability element of the project, and to persuade the development team to implement in keeping with the usability consultant's recommendations. But the project manager must also be sufficiently technical in order to bolster persuasion with consistent technical reasoning when the development team present obstacles or objections of a technical nature.

Designing web-sites to suit diverse international markets and cultures is now accepted as good business practice. It illustrates that the organization responsible for the site is sensitive to local needs. Unfortunately for Rural Net, the original idea in the EU proposal was to produce a pan European site with a standard template which would be used by all similar projects running in four different countries. The UK content providers wanted something that was tailored specifically to the requirements of their users. In the end this was achieved but it did cause delays in the project work.

The Beginning of Progress: Common Sense and Consistency

The catalyst for change occurred when the project missed some deadlines which put its funding in jeopardy. At this stage one of the industrial sponsors,

Telco, assigned a small team to work on Rural Net and helped to pull it around. This team provided project management and development skills. Their work involved liasing with all the project partners and making some common sense improvements to a site prototype.

The Telco team (especially the project manager) understood that people expect Web conventions to be fairly standard and become resentful and confused when this is not the case. So actions (verbs) on the original button bar were replaced with categories (nouns) – *education, tourism, business, community, transport, training*. This meant that users could search for information using hypertext links in a way that was familiar to them from its use in other web-sites. More importantly for naïve users it provides an analogy that is similar to the categorisation used in printed material, such as magazines, books and newspapers.

This version of the interface made great improvements to the navigation of site, providing a use of language which was more in tune with prospective users. It illustrated that usable web-sites can be created by following some very basic rules. For example: making sure that users can access all the functions of the site all of the time. The layout of horizontal content topics button bar (underneath the header) and vertical functions button bar (to the left side of the screen) ensured that users could navigate their way around the site without needing to scroll and that the options available to them were always visible. These comments may seem obvious, but the briefest of excursions on to the web will show that too few designers show consistency in their use of navigational constructs. They do not consider the needs people have for visual metaphors, for example, the web page as an electronic version of the magazine or catalogue.

The First Usability Review

By this time there were two prototypes of the site, the original and Telco's improved version. So far no formal usability work had been carried out. It was at this stage that the author was employed to provide usability consultancy. The aim was to provide impartial advice, in the form of a review of the work carried out, which would hopefully be acceptable to all parties. The project had reached a difficult stage. The usability consultant is often a sympathetic ear for conflicting opinions or long harboured grievances. Frustration with the site was such that a representative of one of the content providers confided that they would not trust a particular designer to paint their garden shed.

The benefit of working as an external usability consultant is that one's views are usually accepted, without question, as impartial. If you are professional and tailor your work to the needs of your client, it is not difficult to get respect. However, it is much harder to push through change, when you are not part of the project team. The requirements of the Rural Net project dictated a fast turn around, so the usability consultancy consisted of expert reviews of the site plus liaison with project partners to help facilitate change. Much of this liaison consisted of trying to persuade the technical lead to accept the user friendly changes that had already been implemented by the Telco team.

Expert reviews are a "discount" usability method (Nielsen, 1994), which can be useful when there is neither time nor budget to carry out tests with users. Research has shown that expert reviews are effective in identifying faults, even a worst case assessment believes that they identify 50 per cent of all usability faults, which can make a major impact on many sites (Cuomo and Bowen, 1994). Heuristic evaluations are cheap and they are efficient, so why are they not used more? In the case of Rural Net, even though the problems were identified and the partners were happy with the results of the review, changes were slow in coming. From experience the reason seems to be that designers and developers are not prepared to accept the findings of an expert review (Teasley and Scholtz, 1997). Grudin (1991) says that a problem with many products is that their developers are not "forced to see the pain they cause" and this is the real value of user testing.

Progress in Usability: Achieving Clarity and Focus

By focusing on specific faults and their solutions, a certain amount of progress was made. Visual appeal, site and page level branding were improved, and all partners were in general agreement about the direction and purpose of the site. Originally it had not been clear at whom the Rural Net site was aimed. The use of a simple header improved the situation (previous versions of the site had no header). Navigation was much improved, firstly by ensuring that all major topics were always viewable (even when the browser was resized), and secondly, by promoting the principle of breadth rather depth in relation to topic headings. This meant that more categories were permanently viewable and the organization of their sub topics was improved in terms of logic and the provision of cross indexing. An adequate search facility was still required.

A major navigational problem which remained was the fact that every time a user clicked a link to an external site a new window was opened. User testing has shown this to be a serious problem for naïve users who do not realise the context in which they find themselves or how to get back to the original site. In addition, the button bars on Rural Net did not look like obviously clickable links. It was recommended that they be replaced by 3D button style links which naïve users perceive more easily as objects that can be clicked (Vora and Helander 1997).

Two requirements from the original EU specification for the site needed to be considered: personalization and a map style application. It was felt that personalization was a valuable attribute for regular users, but the way in which it was presented with the implication that all users must register to access the site would discourage many potential visitors. Consequently, the apparently mandatory login was replaced with an invitation for "regular users" to login, plus access to information about regular user (personalization) options on the home page. The idiosyncratic map style application provided in previous versions of the site was discarded.

Often after a usability consultant has been engaged there is an initial push to improve a web-site and put the end users first. However, after a while inertia can set in and conflicting aims and ideas for the site resurface. By the time sponsorship for the author's consultancy ended there were two prototype web-sites: Telco's, which had implemented most of the usability improvements, and the official development site which had not. This situation was not as negative as it sounds, the essence of usability is to concentrate on key improvements, in this case it was a navigational structure which users could understand. The usability work also gave support to some of the key changes negotiated by the Telco project manager.

Lessons Learned

Usability consultants frequently experience déjà vu. Many of the lessons learnt on Rural Net have occurred on other projects, before and since. In relation to Rural Net there are two lessons which had particular significance:

- *The need for understandable topic headings in order to navigate a web-site.* People are reliant on clear and appropriate topic headings as an initial introduction to the content of the site and subsequently as their guide (combined with *Search*) to navigation of the site. Obscure headings and use of complex language frustrate users and cause them to desert a site as quickly as they accessed it.

- *The importance of good project management.* Good technical project management is an essential ingredient in ensuring the usability of a web-site. The project management method should be designed to produce software, not to fill paper. Many of the usability improvements carried out on Rural Net were pushed through by a sympathetic and highly professional project manager provided by Telco. Unfortunately, the influence of this project manager was limited and many project decisions on Rural Net were made by committee.

Other lessons which frequently arise when attempting to improve the usability of a web-site with many stakeholders, were also found in the Rural Net project.

- A usability review can identify many of the faults of a web-site, rapidly and efficiently. But it does not mean that anyone will act on the recommendations of the report.

- *There is no substitute for testing with real users.* The problem with discount methods like heuristic evaluation is not their lack of effectiveness but their lack of impact on the people who are responsible for implementing changes to the web-site (Lauesen 1997).

- *Usability work on a prototype will save time and money.* The earlier you carry out some sort of usability work the more time and money you will save.

- *Do not expect to be thanked for being right.* Although not ideal, it can make life much easier if the people you work with (clients, designers, developers) believe they came up with the ideas for usability improvements themselves.

- *New technology and old bureaucracy do not mix.* Do not underestimate the power of bureaucracy and the "but that's how we always do it" mentality. They have been around for a long time, and can override the best and most practical usability suggestions.

- *Facilitation, persuasion and selling skills are just as important as HCI knowledge.* It is one thing knowing what needs to be changed to improve a web-site, it is quite another to get people to do it.

- *Prioritise usability improvements.* There will never be the time, budget or commitment to carry out a range of usability improvements, so pick the most important ones and do your best to make sure that they are implemented.

- *Learn to live with some level of unusability.* Be realistic, even the best web-sites have some unusable features.

- *The amount of usability improvement will be in inverse relation to the amount of money that has so far been spent.* If considerable expense has been put into developing unusable technologies, designs etc., it is unlikely that usability findings will lead to their being ditched immediately.

- *No one sets out to produce an unusable web-site.* Most developers and designers want to produce sites that deliver a good user experience. However, they often have unrealistic views concerning the users requirements and level of skill. For example, they believe that users are as interested in new technology and special effects as they are (this explains the current preponderance of slow Flash sites). Whereas most users only want to complete their online task as quickly and easily as possible.

References

Cuomo DL and Bowen CD (1994) Understanding Usability Issues Addressed by Three User-System Interface Evaluation Techniques, Interacting with Computers, 6(1):86–108

Grudin J (1991) Systematic sources of sub-optimal design in large product development organizations, Human-Computer Interaction 6, pp 147–196

Guardian ICM Survey (January 2001)

Lauesen S (1997) Usability Engineering in Industrial Practice, Interact '97, Chapman & Hall, London.

Nielsen J (1994) Usability Engineering, Academic Press

Rosenfeld L and Morville P (1998) Information Architecture for the World Wide Web. O'Reilly

Teasley B and Scholtz J (1997) User-Centred GUI Standards Design: A Case Study, Interact '97. Chapman & Hall

Vora PR and Helander MG (1997) Hypertext and its Implications for the Internet, Handbook of Human-Computer Interaction. Elsevier Science

Strategies to Make E-Business More Customer-Centered

Richard Anderson and Jared Braiterman

Building user-centered business and experience design practices in the unpredictable world of digital business requires diplomacy, flexibility and, above all, creativity. In this chapter, we share our experiences of working within small and large organizations which were trying to "add" customer experience research and testing to e-business design and engineering. Working in leadership positions in four professional services firms and a digital startup, we have found that transforming e-business development practices requires understanding the specifics of each organization – and also stretching the methods and principles of human-computer interaction (HCI).

A Constantly Changing Backdrop

Within four digital business service firms and a digital startup, we have found that our work has included traditional usability projects but has often gone beyond those boundaries. We have contributed to strategy, design and technology projects where usability is not important at all. If usability is understood as standardized interfaces, ease of learning, or efficiency in finding information, many real world web projects intentionally violate these practices. For audiences like early adopters and youth markets, uniqueness and newness are often essential brand ingredients.

We believe that "experience" captures the concept of user interaction with digital media better than "usability" though there are shortcomings even with that term. We not only design experiences and interfaces, but also apply user-centered methods and principles to create new businesses and products. It is equally uncertain that "user" is always the best word for us; sometimes we have found other terms more appropriate, including "customer," "experiencer," "consumer" and "actor." As we stress throughout this chapter, organization and context affect everything, including the very terms we use to describe our work and its audiences.

Changing market conditions as well as the specific core expertise and cultures of our organizations determine the context of what we do as advocates for the end user. From the web's boom to its recent bust, we have encountered changing opportunities and obstacles. In a period of rapid acquisitions and spin-offs, we have been fortunate to gain the perspective of working at small, medium and large organizations. While all these organizations have played leading roles in creating and transforming the web, they differ markedly in expertise and culture. Many professional service firms rightly claim expertise in design, strategy, and technology, but their histories are often weighted greater in one area than others.

Both time-to-market pressures and large scale web-sites' requirement for multidisciplinary teams challenge old-style, purist approaches to usability. The pressure of "Internet time" demands flexibility and creativity in crafting research plans and implementing findings. Multi-disciplinary teams can include information architects, graphic designers, product managers, functional analysts, business strategists, technologists, marketers and engineers. Creating new online experiences requires heterogeneous skills and perspectives. We have found that customer advocacy is most effective when we or our perspectives inform teams from the initial formulation of business strategy through concept, design and development. Gone are the guru critiques of bad usability, with long lead times for research and comfortable distance from the product. Instead, we find ourselves simultaneously changing how organizations build e-businesses and bringing customer focus to our clients and products. At the e-business organizations where we have worked, we find that collaboration, compromise, and longer-term perspectives are imperative.

In today's climate where the path to profitability has become the key e-business metric, we find continued and even increased interest in HCI principles and observational research to uncover customer behavior, site shortcomings and innovative solutions. While e-business leaders increasingly come to professional service firms dedicated to "usability," an equal number come with misconceptions about the value and role of research-based customer experience. Whether through focus groups or quantitative log analysis software, some e-businesses feel they already know their customers and have designed for their needs. Others consider usability something to address only in the design phase, after business plans and strategies are already set in place.

In e-business, the "political" challenges for usability and customer advocacy vary greatly. Our intent in this chapter is to describe strategies and practices that worked, and allude to some that didn't work. We also provide some insight about how to make the most out of diverse organizations and shifting market conditions for e-business.

A Variety of Organizations and Contexts

It has been a wild ride in the world of the web from boom, where business models and profitability didn't matter, to bust, where the opposite became true very quickly. During the late 1990s boom, e-business user experience was championed almost exclusively by a small number of brand and design visionaries. With the downturn, usability and user experience is far more widely seen as critical to increasing revenue and business success. During the boom, service firms could pick and choose clients since demand far outpaced supply for e-services. Post-boom, service firms have been forced to look for and uniquely appeal to clients, increasingly through claims of customer focus. This rapid shift has affected the politics of usability dramatically.

We have worked for five e-business organizations with unique histories and challenges. One was just six months old, while two firms were long established and pre-dated the rise of e-business by roughly ten years. Our organizations' core expertise ranged widely from strategy to engineering, and from systems integration to design. The tremendous shift in market conditions has affected all of the companies, their clients and end users. And since designing clients' business offerings dramatically reveals their organizational structures, we have an even broader understanding of the changing context of e-business.

(Note that we have chosen to use pseudonyms rather than the actual organization names in order that the reader identify with the range of organizational types rather than the specifics of any company.)

High Design

High Design is our code name for a very successful, mid-sized Internet brand and design firm with offices in three cities, international projects, a highly respected design guru, and over 200 employees when we began work with them in the late 1990s. High Design's history and practice were solidly rooted in effective communication and branding, an expertise that enabled it to make a successful transition from highly praised print to digital design firm.

High Design carried over key elements of its design practices from print to digital. After rigorous internal critiques, High Design teams routinely presented three design directions to its clients for input and choice. Involving actual users was not a natural step, though its leadership and practitioners believed and touted their process as highly user-centered. In fact when we arrived, information architects, graphic designers and brand strategists already considered themselves champions of the "user experience".

The challenge was adding customer research and testing to an organization that already believed it was providing for the "user experience" and had already been successful for many years. The nature of the organization encouraged us to partner with and support designers and the design process. Rather than look strictly at efficiency and tasks, we brought a holistic approach to user experience in specific, unique projects. And we took a gradual approach to incorporating the desirable involvement of users.

The Integrator

The Integrator is a successful web consultancy, with offices in more than 15 cities on four continents and approximately 2500 employees. It offers full-service Internet strategy, design, and implementation services. Prior to the late 1990s, the Integrator provided information technology services as a systems integrator, and acquired its design competency through the acquisition of mid-sized design firms.

We became part of the Integrator through one such acquisition. We faced the challenges of shifting from a design to a technology core expertise in an organization that also had already been successful with its previous practices. Its culture offered everyone equal say in a consensus model. The customer face of technology was a novel challenge for the Integrator, and our role involved educating and scaling for what appeared at the time to be limitless growth. Ultimately, the Integrator's leadership chose to increase its user research department through yet another acquisition, and we chose to join many of the designers in leaving.

Aqua Studio

Aqua Studio is a flourishing, one city web design firm founded and staffed with seasoned professionals, many of whom had left larger consultancies. Aqua Studio focused on design excellence and found a niche working on boutique projects under the radar of larger global web services firms. Aqua Studio weathered the economic downturn in part by its portfolio of unique and compelling designs and in part by articulating a customer-centered strategy at all stages of site design and re-design.

One of us joined Aqua Studio in its first year and helped it grow and double in size. Fluctuating client demand and its small size made it imperative to train others in conducting research and testing when projects swelled. Conversely when business waned, the focus shifted from direct research to business development, contributing to the design of Aqua Studio's own site and working with the principals to articulate its experience design vision.

The E-Business Builder

The E-Business Builder is a successful, full-service Internet strategy, design, and implementation firm similar to the Integrator, but smaller and younger. Its e-business approach derived from different roots, a combination of technology and business strategy, with strategy leading most client engagements. Whereas the label "experience design" is compelling in design cultures, "experience strategy" more accurately reflects the emphasis needed to bring customer perspectives and involvement to the earliest stages of e-business plan and strategy development. And in contrast to the Integrator, the E-Business Builder did not plan to add a separate user experience department. Multiple roles, few boundaries and sharing are key cultural values; everyone is empowered. In this environment, providing discipline leadership was not readily supported by announcements of responsibility or the granting of resources and authority. Improving attention to customer experience initially involved coaching, advising and educating, and making it clear how business success relies on the involvement of customers and target users in the process.

The Digital Startup

The Digital Startup is a well-funded young company weathering the financial market's embrace and skepticism about consumer oriented e-businesses.

147

Its core expertise lies in engineering, networks, storage and databases. Nonetheless, in its first two years there was executive commitment to customer experience in terms of site performance, ease of use and product development.

The Digital Startup was fortunate to have a talented in-house interaction, design and web development team in the products groups working with engineers, product managers, the founders, marketers, and database specialists. It also hired an outside firm to help with rebranding the site. Becoming "the client" provided a different perspective on the agency-client relationship. The outside agency's lack of customer-centered design practice required in-house elaboration of a functional spec detailing each screen, which was the result of in-house iterative testing of paper sketches, wire frames and designed pages. In addition to written documentation, alliances with key internal marketing directors ensured that the agency corrected problems identified in testing with the home page, the new customer experience and multi-step applications.

Making it easy for tech novices to order products means removing obstacles to transactions, and is a frequent case of our role aligning customer and business goals. One strives to engineer simplicity and fun for the customer, and at the same time design experiences that contribute to business revenue. In addition to customer's subjective evaluations, computer and family press awards, we are also accountable for conversion rates, product sales goals and growth metrics.

Unfortunately, the Experience Design/User Interface group did not survive its venture capitalists' demands and was eliminated in the second round of layoffs in 2001. This unexpected change raises two questions. Can the Digital Startup's profit targets be met with engineer-driven products? And how, in a technology-centric organization, can you convince executives and investors that customer-centered product development is of equal importance to engineering, databases, networks and storage?

Starting in the Middle and Working Our Way Backward and Forward Simultaneously

What do you do when called into a large scale project midway through website development? How can you transform imperfect situations into opportunities to teach internal teams about ideal HCI practices throughout the product cycle, while still delivering greater customer focus for your client?

At High Design, the obstacles were many – minimal precedent, considerable resistance from designers who were comfortable with earlier work processes, challenges with business development not adequately scoping our work, and demands from clients to rush web-sites to launch. The result was being called into projects after discovery and definition phases were completed, and being asked to "do something." We responded with creativity, flexibility, and a long-term strategy for building an HCI practice.

Designers were unanimous in seeking concept testing, but did not have a clear idea about what that would entail. Some account managers viewed our role as preference testing (i.e. asking customers which one of three alternatives do they prefer). Team by team, we educated within High Design about our role, the insights and design opportunities that could be derived from observational research, the importance of understanding current online and offline customer behavior, and the need for iterative prototyping.

In an early situation, despite assurances that a giant Printer client knew its customers, we designed tests that evaluated three concepts and the three segment, target audience's purchase and decision-making behavior. Despite the Printer's Marketing Department's assurance that its customers are in fact segmented into soho, mid sized company and enterprise, we found that no printer purchasers, whether at large or small businesses, wanted to be categorized by market type in order to view products. Forcing upfront identification with marketing categories, in fact, made customers think that they were being outsmarted and limited in what they could see. Customer research allowed us to revise the web experience and focus not on customer segment but on customers' needs for sorting and comparing products based on functions like printing, scanning, copying and faxing. And the team learned that future projects should engage our expertise and the clients' customers earlier in the process to shape rather than "validate" concept formation.

Working within the same organization over time facilitates the process of improving attention to user experience, with customer discovery shifting to occur parallel to initial business analysis, followed by iterative development of concepts and designs. At the E-Business Builder, the success of an experience design project that involved customers via in-home visits and paper prototyping sessions made it easier to introduce rapid ethnography into a project focused on developing business strategy. At the Integrator, a client content with conventional market research methods wanted more up-front discovery research in future work after they observed some of our customer research sessions on the same day they observed their conventional focus groups. At the Digital Startup, what began as a disaster check two weeks prior to the launch of the original site developed into a full-fledged and highly integrated experience design practice that helped determine product roll-out schedules, onsite interactions and customer experience with a complex application.

Developing Organizational Strategy and Capability: Departments or Distributed Expertise?

What do you do when you are given responsibility to develop an organization's strategy and capability for involving users in the process, but that responsibility is not adequately supported? Is what you do much different than if that responsibility is accompanied by organizational support? How might organizational culture affect the strategy you develop?

At the E-Business Builder, a culture emphasizing collaboration, full participation and minimal hierarchy, responsibility for developing organizational strategy was not supported with a designation of resources, authority, or even an internal announcement of the role. Despite an increasing awareness within the company of the need to involve customers much more extensively, the role remained unofficial and largely unarticulated until the economic high-tech downturn began to prompt high-level steps to publicize it and make experience strategy a key platform for attracting clients.

At High Design, responsibility was accompanied by explicit organizational support, but another unique obstacle remained. One of us was invited to bring his expertise into the company and to form, staff, and develop a new discipline, and that leadership role was announced not only internally but also externally via press release and the firm's web-site. However, becoming effective meant challenging the organization's firm belief that it was already user-centered. The commitment to delivering high quality user experience was already enshrined in its marketing materials and the company's own brand. Designers felt strongly that they thought hard about users and tried to take their perspective into their designs; however, their work practice rarely involved customers well or at all.

Despite disparate situations, the approaches taken were very similar. Initial progress was achieved by working with teams project by project. Ongoing formal and informal sessions were arranged with large numbers of individuals and roles, in addition to project teams, to discuss their work and ways greater attention to customer experience might affect it, and to contrast this with how previous project work had involved users, if at all. Closely working with personnel in the context of project and daily work was key to the development of longer-term strategy.

At the E-Business Builder, the early focus included coaching existing teams to create "it works here" success cases while highlighting previous project work that involved users in desirable ways, even if only in small ways. (Excluding any interested parties or not referencing others' past related work proved to be politically inadvisable.) Personnel who were members of coached project teams then went on to other projects and proceeded to coach their new team members themselves. These and related efforts evolved into the generation of an organizational strategy focused on the evolution of existing roles via continued coaching and other support activities.

At High Design, we built a mid-sized department of cultural anthropologists, usability specialists, and information designers, and faced the challenge of integrating a new role into existing teams and work processes. Because our discipline shared the "user experience" with other disciplines, our new activities involving customers were designed to provide guidance, direction and inspiration to previously existing roles without threatening to take control.

At both firms, divergent experience strategies led to full integration of research, strategy and design, with variations appropriate to each context.

Whether an organization chooses to create a department of specialists or a more distributed expertise, an evolutionary strategy for changing e-business strategy, design and decision making will often be a necessity (Anderson, 2000). Even with executive commitment, it takes time to change established work practices; lots of complex factors need to come together (Dray and Siegel, 1998). Developing an effective organizational strategy ultimately requires patience and learning about the culture and existing work practices of your organization.

Collaborating with Peers and Clients

In the wild world of digital business, collaboration with peers and clients has been critical to our success. Unlike some who have argued to the contrary, attending to user needs and desires must be the responsibility of all team members, not just a subset. Ownership of all components of the process should not be equally shared, since not all share the necessary expertise. But all need to play roles in user research, participate in the analysis and experience modeling activities, and apply what is learned to the businesses and business offerings we design. Approaches that prevent collaboration and require handoffs of findings between disciplines or combining independently generated deliverables at the end do not work well.

At High Design, a couple of design directors were initially resistant to our involvement, fearing the loss of their ability to be creative and in control. At The Integrator, one group of highly independent business consultants was particularly resistant, preferring to do things on their own and as they had done them in the past. On another project, a user research specialist was resistant to alternative interpretations of user data from team members, arguing that only she could interpret user behavior properly. In yet another, a final client decision maker who did not participate in the work overruled results despite unanimous buy-in by the team of consultants and client personnel who did participate in the work. At the Digital Startup, the outside agency working on site re-branding refused to participate in test sessions and initially sought to attribute unwanted findings to "bad users." Obstacles can be formidable.

Successfully "evolving" established work practices requires ongoing learning of other participants' perspectives, ongoing tailoring of activities in view of these perspectives, and ongoing education of all involved. The alternative is to risk being misunderstood by or insulting those you work with or for, which is not at all conducive to effective process change. There is no universal language or translator, only particular environments, teams and organizations. However, collaboration in a process involving users is usually the most powerful communicator.

At High Design, designers were eager to participate in up-front ethnographic research, and their active participation in these early stages made them more open to later concept and design testing. Designers became active researchers observing teenage boys at home playing video games for one project, extreme sports enthusiasts at surf shops and skate parks for another, busy professionals at home and at work attending to meal planning and preparation in yet another. And we insisted that designers' input and interpretation were critical to forming character profiles. Since the profiles were collaboratively created, it was easier to use them later in the project as a guide to design and as an evaluation tool for site strategy and implementation. Active participation in research, interpretation and analysis helped overcome designers' fears that testing is about polling and taking away control and creativity. Training non-experts distributes the work involved and recasts experience research from constraint to inspiration.

At the E-Business Builder, everyone on select multi-disciplinary teams was declared to be a "cultural anthropologist." Teams were split up, equipped with guidance, cameras, and tape recorders, and sent into homes to learn how people relate to their personal media, into workplaces to learn how employees collaborate or try to, etc. (project foci varied). Participation dramatically changed team members' perceptions of target user behavior and needs, generated key insights for online opportunities, and dramatically increased hunger for expanding research activities on future projects. Related effects were achieved via involving most members of multi-disciplinary teams in concept and design development sessions involving users. An added benefit: roles that had previous difficulty working together were able to work together much more effectively and efficiently.

Note that bringing clients and inexperienced teams into direct contact with customers must be managed well. In informal testing without the benefit of a lab's two-way mirror separating observers from the action, we have had to train and at times correct clients when they have behaved improperly. Under pressure to produce desirable results, clients can make research participants uncomfortable. More often, we have seen clients eager to educate and instruct customers in how to use their products. Making effective use of client and non-expert participation requires upfront education about research roles, especially the idea that communication and learning should always be from the customer to the team, along with occasional interventions to keep research on track.

Shifting Tactics from Boom to Bust

Our leadership roles in experience strategy have spanned the "new economy" boom and the "next economy" bust. In addition to specific constraints and opportunities unique to every organization, market conditions greatly affect the politics of usability. During the boom, many traditional companies and web startups hurried to get in on the action. Being "first to market" led to a rush to launch and became a mantra for e-business leaders and their venture capital funders. Working in "Internet time" meant that anything that could slow launch was often suspect. In some cases, that made attention to customer experience prone to be chopped, despite a few loud voices about the perils of ignoring customer experience. Visionary designers and organizations sought to fully integrate experience strategy into their process. And, to protect this "added" expertise from being sacrificed, some service firms – including Aqua Studio – sometimes omitted customer research and testing from project scope and instead carried it out below the radar. Fast, integrated and flexible approaches were most valued.

153

During the bust, clients have become very conservative. Getting it right before getting it out there matters more, and clients now use the word usability before we do – some even have processes that service firms must adhere to. But conservatism means smaller budgets, so we still face enormous pressure to do things quickly. We must also negotiate with and persuade clients who come to us with a "usability plan" that a checklist or generic program may not be best suited to their business problem.

In short, we have gone from "hide it" to "expose it" in terms of how "usability" becomes integrated in e-business strategy and product development. Yet challenges remain in educating our organizations and our clients about best practices throughout the business development cycle. The present atmosphere of shrinking budgets and limited resources make the hiring spree of past years seem a distant memory and reinforces the need for flexibility, collaboration and creativity.

Lessons Learned

What are the basic lessons to be distilled from these experiences in the wild world of digital business?

Go Beyond Old-Style Purist Approaches To Attending To Usability

Standard recipes of attending to "usability" will often be inadequate to specific organizations, projects and contexts. Plus, some of our most valuable work extends beyond usability – including using customer-centered activities early so that we contribute to business strategy and plans, and extending concept and design research to attend to brand experience and self-directed exploration.

Attending to customer experience in the wild world of e-business presents challenges to traditional HCI methods. Unlike productivity applications, e-commerce sites frequently involve new or novice computer users, voluntary participation and unfamiliar ways of shopping, trading, sharing and forming community. Earlier HCI specialists, influenced by experimental and cognitive psychology, emphasized controlled variables and specified tasks. Unlike conventional office productivity, web customer experience is often user-driven, open ended and unpredictable. In place of labs, observational research now happens in customers' own environments, including homes, offices and leisure venues. Flexible methods are needed to address existing offline behavior and to evaluate possible online interactions.

154

Respect and Value the Perspectives of Your Colleagues and Clients

The multidisciplinary nature of large scale web development highlights the need for user-centered design activities to be carried out with the active participation of the whole team, including visual designers, information architects, business strategists, product managers, marketers, engineers and executive leadership. Including non-researchers in planning studies, interviewing and observing prospective users, and analysing research findings fosters greater acceptance of research findings and sparks unique insights brought by team members with diverse expertise.

Be Willing To Be Creative

Specific organizations, changing market conditions, and limited resources suggest that there will always be a gap between ideal practice and possible practice. A cookie cutter approach ignores specific challenges and opportunities unique to all of our situations. In addition to what you bring to your organizations, solicit ideas from others in your company and create an environment that fosters idea generation. Be willing to experiment.

Make Attention To User Experience a Key Part of Your Organization's Brand

It's easy to spend all of your time working at the team level, educating, training and creating success stories. You also need to convince your organization's leadership that customer experience is an essential brand attribute. Such corporate branding will smooth your path, both in working internally and in selling your company's offerings.

Develop an Understanding of the Culture of Your Own Organization

To really know how to handle its political issues, you must understand what drives your organization, its values and goals (Mayhew, 1999). Just as important as gathering a full understanding of customers for new e-businesses experience design and business strategy, you need to conduct research in your own organization and understand how your work can contribute to its business objectives. As Rohn argues, you must practice user-centered design on your own organization (Anderson, 2000). Fortunately, the techniques we use to understand customers can also help us understand our organizations.

Develop an Understanding of Yourself and Your Own Biases

Your success or lack thereof will emerge from the interaction of your background, expertise and limitations with those of your organization. Don't exclude yourself from the process of understanding your organization. Depending on your situation, you may find that in addition to usability know-how, you'll also need to learn more about information visualization, or merchandizing, venture capital funding, field research methods and the path to profitability. And learn how to invite productive collaboration that maximizes the potential of experience strategy experts and non-experts who bring complimentary skills and knowhow.

References

Anderson R (interviewer and editor) (2000) Organizational limits to HCI: A conversation with Don Norman and Janice Rohn, interactions 7(3) (May–June 2000): 36–60

Anderson RI (2000) Making an e-business conceptualization and design process more "user"-centered, interactions 7(4) (July–August 2000):27–30

Dray SM and Siegel DA (1998) User-centered design and the "vision thing", interactions 5(2) (March–April 1998):16–20

Mayhew DJ (1999) Strategic development of the usability engineering function, interactions 6(5) (September–October 1999):27–33

Index

PRACTITIONER SERIES

Series Editor: Ray Paul
Editorial Board: Frank Bott, Nic Holt,
                   Kay Hughes, Elizabeth Hull,
                   Richard Nance, Russel Winder and Sion Wyn

These books are written
by practitioners for practitioners.

They offer thoroughly practical hands-on advice on how to tackle specific problems.
So, if you are already a practitioner in the development, exploitation or management
of IS/IT systems, or you need to acquire an awareness and knowledge of principles
and current practice in an IT/IS topic fast then these are the books for you.

All books in this series will be clear, concise and problem solving and will cover a
wide range of areas including:
● systems design techniques
● performance modelling
● cost and estimation control
● software maintenance
● quality assurance
● database design and administration
● HCI
● safety critical systems
● distributed computer systems
● internet and web applications
● communications, networks and security
● multimedia, hypermedia and digital libraries
● object technology
● client-server
● formal methods
● design approaches
● IT management

All books are, of course, available from all good booksellers (who can order them
even if they are not in stock), but if you have difficulties you can contact the
publishers direct, by telephoning +44 (0) 1483 418822 (in the UK & Europe),
+1/212/4 60/15 00 (in the USA), or by emailing orders@svl.co.uk

www.springer.de www.springer-ny.com

PRACTITIONER SERIES

Developing
IT Staff

A Practical Approach

Mary Clarkson

Developing IT Staff provides an easy reference and down-to-earth practical advice for those who need to tackle the important issues of training and skill development in the context of technical software development jobs.

In this book, Mary Clarkson uses real examples from her experiences as a technical specialist and as an IT training manager, giving practical guidance on how to get people started on their skill development, as well as how to support them through their learning process.

Topics covered include:

- Identifying the real training need and finding solutions
- Choosing an appropriate training method
- Supporting the learning process
- Continuous professional development, with particular relevance to an IT department
- Evaluation (what needs to be evaluated, why and when)
- Technical Skill Assessment

Here is a book that puts training into the context of technical software development jobs.

216 pages
Softcover
ISBN: 1-85233-433-9

Please see page 163 for ordering details

www.springer.de www.springer-ny.com

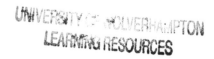